BILLION DOLLAR
BLIND$POT

What is Your Workplace Culture Costing You?

HACIA ATHERTON, CPA, MAPP

SILVERSMITH
PRESS

Published by Silversmith Press–Houston, Texas
www.silversmithpress.com

ISBN 978-1-967386-13-0 (Softcover Book)
ISBN 978-1-967386-16-1 (eBook)

To the leaders who have
the courage to look inward:
Thank you for turning self-awareness into strategy,
and blind spots into bold moves.

Contents

PART 3
Using The Respect Equality Model
To Navigate Workplace Challenges

Introduction

*The cost of silence is often far greater
than the cost of speaking up.*
—Malala Yousafzai.

In the bustling corridors of corporate power, where the rhythm of productivity echoes against the walls of ambition, lies a silent yet formidable foe: poor workplace culture. It's a phenomenon that infiltrates the fabric of far too many organizations, silently eroding productivity, sapping employee morale, and draining financial resources. Leaders tend to focus on the big picture. As a result, we often overlook the profound impact of toxic work environments, dismissing them as mere inconveniences in the pursuit of profit. However, the truth is far more sobering.

Poor workplace culture has a staggering economic toll. It leads to disengagement, increased turnover, and health-related issues, all of which impact how businesses operate. According to the *State of the Global Workplace: 2023 Report* by Gallup, disengaged employees alone cost the U.S. economy an estimated $450-$550 billion annually in lost productivity. This loss is not merely a number; it is a reflection of squandered human potential, deferred dreams, and unfulfilled aspirations.

Beyond Blue, an Australian mental health organization, has helped further identify the profound repercussions of workplace-related mental health issues resulting from poor workplace culture. Their research estimates that untreated mental health conditions exact a toll of around $10.9 billion annually on Australian employers. This is an economic burden that manifests through various channels, including absenteeism, diminished productivity, and increased compensation claims. With these kinds of numbers, it's clear that workplace culture is not just an inconvenient secondary consideration. Organizations and leaders need to prioritize workplace culture initiatives to foster a healthier, more empowering and productive workforce if they want to mitigate these costs.

It's not just a question of increasing efficiency. Stress, burnout, and other mental health issues have become destructively persistent in workplace environments rife with toxicity and fear. The consequences extend far beyond the individual, permeating the organizational ecosystem and manifesting in increased healthcare costs, absenteeism, and decreased productivity, all of which are detrimental to society's corporate bottom line and psychological well-being.

Furthermore, the revolving door of turnover exacts a toll on organizations, both financially and operationally. The costs associated with continually recruiting, onboarding, and training new employees add up quickly, draining resources that could otherwise be allocated to innovation and growth. Moreover, when valuable talent leaves, it disrupts team dynamics, diminishes institutional knowledge, and undermines organizational stability. Let's stop burying our heads in the sand and face facts: as leaders, we are being faced with a significant issue that costs us billions. This demands our immediate attention.

The relentless pursuit of profitability and market dominance means that we often overlook a critical driver of success: diversity and inclusion. McKinsey's seminal reports, *Diversity Wins* and *Diversity Matters*, provide compelling evidence of the profound impact that diverse executive teams and inclusive cultures can have on financial performance. Nevertheless, diversity and inclusion alone are not enough—they're only part of the picture. To unlock their full potential, organizations must foster an environment where diversity, inclusion, and belonging can truly thrive. This requires creating workplaces that prioritize the psychological well-being of all employees, ensuring that individuals feel valued, respected, and empowered to contribute authentically. In other words, it's not enough to make superficial changes. We need to shift the workplace culture overall.

If you think this is a big ask, you're right. But addressing the toxic cultures that persist in many corporations is not just a moral imperative; it's a business necessity. Without action, these cultures undermine the very foundations of collaboration, innovation, and engagement. Organizations that waste time and energy fighting themselves, which don't enable their employees to thrive and do their best, are not organizations that succeed. Leaders must take bold steps to dismantle the barriers that perpetuate exclusion and fear, replacing them with cultures of respect, psychological safety, and genuine inclusion. Only then can they realize the transformative power of their people and drive meaningful, sustainable success.

Consider the stark contrast in outcomes between companies which prioritize gender and racial diversity at the executive level and those that don't. According to McKinsey's research, companies with gender-diverse executive teams are 25% more likely to achieve above-average profitability. Similarly, organizations with diverse racial and ethnic representation are 35% more likely to outperform their industry peers financially. Is anything else in your strategic toolbox likely to give similar results?

When individuals from different backgrounds, experiences, and perspectives come together in an organizational culture that empowers their voices, they bring a wealth of ideas, insights, and approaches to problem-solving. This diversity of thought fuels innovation, drives creativity, and enhances a company's ability to adapt and thrive in an ever-evolving marketplace.

However, despite the clear business case for positive workplace cultures, diversity and inclusion are something many organizations continue to grapple with. Attitudes can be hard to change, and barriers such as unconscious biases and entrenched norms continue to hinder progress. But the costs stemming from inaction are significant, both in terms of missed opportunities and tangible financial losses.

We must first acknowledge the true cost of poor workplace culture, both in dollars and cents and in the human toll it exacts. Only then can we begin to cultivate a new paradigm of leadership, one rooted in empathy, inclusivity, and resilience. Investing in employee engagement, nurturing supportive leadership, and prioritizing a culture of well-being can pave the way for a brighter, more prosperous future where organizations thrive and individuals flourish.

True Inclusion

When anyone talks about fixing toxic corporate culture, many leaders stop listening, because all too often the word "toxic" is followed by "masculinity," along with an initiative which largely involves criticizing masculine behaviors. It's true that many aspects of traditional workplaces are built around male-oriented expectations, and women certainly do face challenges in these environments. But the truth is that men suffer from these expectations and norms as well. What I've come to realize is that true reform involves not a focus on what's wrong, but on better understanding and using the unique strengths that everyone has.

For me, this understanding comes from a place of both empathy and personal experience. As a woman, I've spent much of my career in male-dominated environments, where I often felt compelled to think and act through a traditionally masculine lens. A near-death accident forced me to rebuild my body, mind, and soul, plunging me into a journey of profound self-discovery and transformation. Along this arduous path, I came face-to-face with the suffocating weight of societal expectations and the confining cages that society constructs—not only for men but for women, too.

It was a moment that forever changed the trajectory of my life—a harrowing brush with mortality that thrust me into the University of Hard Knocks. In the aftermath of a near-fatal accident, I found myself grappling not only with physical pain, but also with profound existential questions about the nature of resilience, purpose, and human potential.

I discovered the transformative power of positive psychology amidst the darkness of uncertainty—a beacon of hope that illuminated my path forward.

Through the lens of adversity, I understood that true strength does not lie in the absence of challenges; rather true strength comes from our ability to navigate our challenges with resilience, optimism, and unwavering determination. My journey of healing and self-discovery led me to embrace the principles we explore in this book as we seek to uncover the factors that contribute to humanity's flourishing and well-being. Through a questioning mindset, I began to see the untapped potential within individuals and organizations to create positive change, even in the face of adversity.

Positive psychology focuses on what's called the PERMA framework—Positive Emotions, Engagement, Relationships, Meaning, and Accomplishment. It has widespread applications in leadership, organizational behavior, and workplace culture. I witnessed firsthand the profound impact that a 'strengths-based' approach, grounded in empathy, authenticity, and a growth mindset, can have on individual performance, team dynamics, and organizational success. This realization inspired me to dedicate my life's work to helping leaders harness the power of positive psychology to create thriving, inclusive, and resilient organizations.

In the following pages, we will explore the principles

of positive psychology and their practical applications in driving organizational change. From cultivating a culture of gratitude and resilience, to fostering authentic connections and meaningful engagement, we will uncover the key ingredients for building workplaces where individuals can truly thrive. And I'll share with you my own approach, derived from the PERMA framework and intended as a roadmap for leaders like us: the **Respect Equality Model (REM)**.

REM is the belief that everyone, regardless of gender or background, deserves equal respect and opportunities. This approach fosters an environment where people can learn from one another, appreciating and integrating the strengths of those different from themselves. Respect and empathy are more than passive ideals—they are active choices. To build these cultures, we must first reject the outdated roles and practices that society has imposed on us. Remember that leadership is not about following a prescribed path, but forging your own.

Be the Hero of Your Leadership Journey

Leadership is not a hand-me-down suit that you're forced to wear. It's a role you create, define, and embody authentically. And to lead authentically, you must step into the role of the hero in your own leadership journey. This means waking up to the invisible structures that shape your decisions and questioning whether they align with who you are and what you want to achieve. It means empowering yourself to challenge the status quo and embracing your unique values and vision. It means not just paying lip service to ideas of diversity, but understanding what that means, and stepping up to take charge constructively.

In this book, we'll start with an examination of workplace dynamics, including both masculine and feminine mindsets, strengths, and weaknesses. We'll see how gender roles have been used to shape workplace culture and why. In doing so, we'll uncover how to consciously use and combine the best of each to create an effective workplace culture.

Then we'll explore Positive Psychology and the Respect Equality Model. We'll look at what the PERMA framework entails, how I came to develop REE, and why. After that, we'll look at specific ways you can use these tools in your own organization, transforming not just labels and rules but mindsets in a way that will lead to a more productive and sustainable work environment—one that your employees will succeed in, not just endure.

The courage to break free from outdated practices is not just an act of self-liberation but a commitment to building workplaces where respect, inclusion, and empowerment flourish. This book is your guide to that transformation, equipping you with the tools and insights to question the world as it is and create the world as it could be.

I invite you to join me in this exploration as we apply the principles of positive psychology to personal stories and the fabric of our workplaces. Together, we'll venture towards creating respectful, resilient, inclusive environments, proving that true leadership is about leading courageously against the odds and breaking free from stereotype-induced suffering - lighting the way for future generations to live in a world brimming with equality, confidence, and boundless opportunity. I'll show you how to turn that billion-dollar workplace culture issue into a billion-dollar opportunity by improving engagement, reducing turnover, and driving sustainable organizational success.

Let's get started!

PART 1

The Power and Peril of Gender Norms

Millimeters

We may encounter many defeats,
but we must not be defeated.
—Maya Angelou.

It was a bitter evening in July 2017, and I lay on the cold earth, grappling with a tsunami of searing pain, racing thoughts and wild emotions. The ground beneath me, once just ordinary arena sand, had become the stage of my life's most defining moment. As the ever-intensifying pain surged through my body, and I realized that my legs were completely lifeless, my survival instinct kicked in, and I rolled on to my front and began to fervently army-crawl my way across the arena, to avoid being trampled by the horse I'd just fallen from.

Beyond the extreme physical pain, a more profound ache emerged—the realization of how swiftly everything can change.

I had been in the midst of an intense training session

for my upcoming equestrian competition. This event held the key to my dreams, my chance to secure the qualifying score needed to earn a spot in the prestigious World Equestrian Games. My partner in this pursuit was my magnificent young dressage mare "CC"—600 kilos (1300 lbs) of power and grace.

On this particular night, something unexpectedly shifted within CC during our training session. She had reached her limit, and her response was sudden and unforeseen. In a split second, she reared up vertically, throwing me from her back with unimaginable force. My world turned upside down as I flew through the air and crashed to the ground, and in that same terrifying instant, CC stumbled and her massive frame came crashing down on top of me, shattering my body and my lifelong dream.

My body immediately went into shock and while the pain was excruciating—searing through every fiber of my body and soul, it didn't even feel real. Here I was trapped beneath the weight of my own beloved horse, struggling to breathe yet not even present at the same time. It was like living my worst nightmare and knowing I couldn't wake up.

In that moment, the weight pressing down on me was more than just physical—it was the crushing realization that everything I had built, every dream I had nurtured, had been ripped away. As I lay there in complete disbelief, a profound emptiness consumed me, a void so deep it felt as though it might swallow me whole.

As I lay there, a suffocating fear set in, mingling with the pain. It wasn't just the fear of the injuries or the uncertainty of survival—it was the fear of losing who I was, of becoming someone unrecognizable to myself. I felt completely untethered, adrift in a sea of unanswered questions. The life I had carefully crafted now felt like a distant memory, and the road ahead seemed impossibly long and uncertain.

I was airlifted to the Alfred Hospital in Melbourne, Australia, to face a nine-hour surgery as the best orthopedic surgeons in the state worked tirelessly to put my shattered body back together. As the surgery doors closed behind me, my family was told that mere millimeters dictated the fine line between my life and death.

This revelation brought lucid clarity about my purpose and instilled a deep sense of gratitude for the gift of millimeters—the universe's way of granting me a second chance. This moment of stark realization fueled my determination to create a significant positive impact in the world, driving the motivation behind this book.

My gratitude for this "gift of millimeters" is a testament to the power of second chances and their responsibility, inspiring a journey of personal resilience and meaningful change, particularly in challenging the norms of corporate leadership and championing Respect Equality in male-dominated industries.

This tragedy could either defeat me or propel me forward into a profound transformation. I chose the latter, and in this deep state of vulnerability, I sensed the dawning of a monumental journey that would redefine me as a human being.

This journey was more than a road to physical recovery. It was, and continues to be, a deeper expedition into self-leadership through the darkest of experiences. This moment was my initiation into the University of Hard Knocks, where life's most brutal lessons are taught outside classroom walls. This was my admission into a transformative phase of life. During my recovery, I had to ask some hard questions, "If I've been given this second chance, what am I truly meant to do with it?"

As leaders, we can challenge our perceptions, overcome biases, and approach problems with clarity and openness. By harnessing this superpower, we can navigate complex challenges, inspire our teams, and drive meaningful change in our organizations.

The Ladder of Inference explains how our perceptions, shaped by past experiences and beliefs, influence our actions and decisions. For male executives in male-dominated industries, understanding this model is crucial for leading change towards greater psychological well-being and gender respect. Recognizing and challenging personal and organizational assumptions can help address biases, promote inclusivity, and foster an environment where diverse perspectives are valued. This awareness is essential for creating a culture that supports growth, innovation, and equality, aligning leadership practices with the evolving expectations of today's workforce.

The Ladder of Inference is a powerful concept that helps us understand how we process information, form beliefs, and make decisions. Developed by organizational psychologist Chris Argyris, the Ladder of Inference illustrates the steps we unconsciously take as we move from observed data to action. It consists of the following:

1. Observation
2. Selection
3. Interpretation
4. Assumption
5. Inference
6. Belief
7. Action

At the base of the ladder are the observable facts. These are the raw inputs we receive from the world around us, such as what we see, hear or experience. As we move up the ladder, we selectively interpret and assign meaning to these data points based on our past experiences, cultural background, and personal beliefs.

The next rung of the ladder involves making assumptions. We filter the data through our existing mental models and beliefs, filling in gaps and making inferences to make sense of the information. Our biases, stereotypes, and preconceived notions can influence these assumptions, leading us to interpret the data in a way that aligns with our worldview. From assumptions, we move to concluding. Based on our interpretations and beliefs, we form conclusions about what the data means, and what actions should be taken. These conclusions may not always be based on objective reality, rather on our subjective perceptions and biases. Finally, at the top of the ladder, we act based on our conclusions. These actions can range from small everyday decisions to major strategic moves, all shaped by our underlying beliefs and interpretations of the world.

The spaces between each rung of the Ladder of Inference represent the often-unseen gaps in our reasoning, where assumptions and biases can take root and distort our understanding of reality. These gaps highlight the moments when we transition from observing data to assigning meaning, drawing conclusions, and taking action—moments ripe for misinterpretation if not approached with intentionality.

For example, imagine a leader observing a quiet team

member during a meeting. Without pausing to explore the context, the leader might unconsciously assign meaning to the behavior, assuming the individual is disengaged or unprepared. This assumption could lead to a conclusion that the team member lacks initiative, resulting in actions like excluding them from future high-stakes projects. Over time, such missteps shape organizational culture, fostering environments where employees may feel overlooked or undervalued.

Understanding the ladder's structure invites leaders to question their interpretations and assumptions. Instead of jumping to conclusions, a leader might ask clarifying questions: *"Are there barriers preventing engagement? Does this person process information differently?"* Leaders can uncover deeper truths and build more inclusive, informed decision-making processes by addressing the gaps between rungs with curiosity and openness.

These small, often unnoticed decisions accumulate in organizational culture, defining norms and influencing behaviors. When leaders intentionally examine the gaps in their reasoning, they improve their decision-making and set a precedent for thoughtful, bias-aware leadership that fosters trust, inclusivity, and innovation.

For example, imagine a manager receiving feedback from a team member during a performance review. The manager observes the data (the feedback) and quickly ascends the ladder of inference, making assumptions about the team member's competence based on past interactions or stereotypes. These assumptions lead to conclusions about the team member's abilities, which in turn influence the manager's actions, such as assigning less challenging tasks or withholding growth opportunities.

Over time, repeated patterns of decision-making based on biased assumptions can shape the organization's culture, leading to a lack of trust, communication breakdowns, and diminished morale among team members. By understanding the ladder of inference and actively challenging our perceptions and biases, we can make more informed decisions, foster a culture of inclusivity and equity, and drive positive change within our organizations.

The ladder of inference profoundly impacts how individuals perceive and interpret the world around them, often forming unique perspectives or "truths" about a given situation. These differing perspectives can create a reality for each person involved that may be vastly different from the others, resulting in conflicts, misunderstandings, and missed opportunities for collaboration.

In the days, weeks and months that followed, as I endured the slow and painful path to recovery, I found myself confronting truths I had never faced before. The abrupt and merciless accident was a stark reminder of life's fragility and resilience. I began to see the parallels between my own recovery and the journey of empowered leadership. Just like the intricate process of healing, leading, especially in environments resistant to change, requires patience, determination, and an unwavering belief in the possibility of transformation.

In the early days of my recovery, I was told by doctors that I might never walk independently again without aids. Those words struck me deeply, but I refused to accept them as my fate. With unwavering determination, I stood for the first time, an achievement that felt monumental as I pushed through unimaginable pain to beat the odds. Each step I took thereafter was a testament to the power of facing one's darkest fears with a relentless, no-excuse, never-give-up mindset. The road to recovery was long and fraught with challenges, but I persevered, eventually learning to walk again. Not only did I reclaim my ability to walk, but I also went on to run a half-marathon. This journey taught me that true strength lies in confronting and overcoming adversity. By embracing resilience and determination, we can transcend even the most daunting obstacles, proving that our limits are often just starting points for extraordinary achievements.

Following my accident and the pioneering journey to establish Empowered Women in Trades—a groundbreaking initiative dissolving barriers for women in the skilled trades—I navigated the subtle balance between seizing opportunities and facing uncertainties. This experience illuminated the complexities of where potential and unpredictability intertwine, guiding me through uncharted territories towards creating a more inclusive future in traditionally male-dominated fields.

This melting pot of interwoven dynamics, often steeped in discomfort, reveals itself to be the crucible in which true leadership is forged. Embracing discomfort—as a constant companion rather than a transient challenge—has been pivotal in my personal and professional evolution. This realization underscores a critical message for leaders, especially in male-dominated industries: the greatest opportunities often lie hidden within the folds of uncertainty. To lead effectively, champion gender respect, and cultivate a culture of high psychological well-being, one must first learn to stand firm in the face of discomfort. Here, in the discomfort of challenging deeply rooted stereotypes and advocating for change, we find our most profound opportunities for growth and transformation. This book delves into embracing uncertainty and discomfort as pathways to empowerment, urging leaders to view these experiences not as barriers but as gateways to unparalleled leadership success.

As I charted my way back to health, I simultaneously mapped out a new path for leadership, one that embraces the core values of positive psychology, where fostering positive emotions is not a sign of weakness, rather, it's a strategy for building resilience and driving engagement. Creating meaningful relationships in the workplace goes beyond networking into forming the foundation for a supportive and collaborative culture.

This chapter is more than recounting a life-altering event; it is the beginning of a discourse on transformational leadership. It sets the groundwork for exploring how the tenets of positive psychology can be applied in corporate leadership, particularly in industries where change is both necessary and challenging. As you read through these pages, my hope is that my story resonates with you, not just as a tale of survival but as a testament to the power of positive change, resilience, and the indomitable human spirit.

Reflecting on this transformative journey, it becomes clear that the lessons learned during my recovery extend far beyond the personal sphere. The principles of resilience, patience, and unwavering determination are just as vital in the professional realm, particularly in today's rapidly evolving and competitive landscape. My experiences underscore organizations' need to foster environments of paramount excellence, trust, respect, and well-being. These elements are not just nice-to-haves; they are crucial for attracting and nurturing diverse talent in an era marked by a fierce war for talent.

In my recovery, the support and encouragement

of my medical team and loved ones were instrumental. Similarly, a workplace that fosters psychological safety and mutual respect empowers individuals to take risks, innovate, and thrive. Leaders must create spaces where employees feel valued, heard, and supported. This involves actively promoting diversity and inclusion, ensuring that every team member can bring their authentic selves to work without fear of judgment or exclusion.

Moreover, my journey taught me the value of small, incremental progress. Just as each step in my physical recovery was a milestone, in professional settings, recognizing and celebrating small victories can build momentum and drive sustained success. Encouraging a growth mindset, where challenges are viewed as opportunities for development rather than insurmountable obstacles, can transform organizational culture and performance.

The parallels between personal resilience and professional success are profound. By embracing the principles of resilience, patience, and a never-give-up attitude, organizations can navigate change more effectively and foster a culture of excellence and innovation. Just as my journey from immobility to running a half-marathon was marked by determination and support, so too can organizations achieve remarkable outcomes by cultivating an environment where trust, respect, and well-being are foundational.

My recovery journey is not just about overcoming

physical limitations; it is a profound testament to the power of the human spirit and the importance of supportive environments. By translating these personal learnings into a professional context, leaders can build workplaces that excel in performance and nurture their employees' holistic well-being. This holistic approach is essential for thriving in today's competitive landscape and for ensuring long-term success and sustainability.

As we conclude "Millimeters," it's clear that my personal narrative of overcoming a near-fatal equestrian accident, culminating in the triumphant achievement of running a half-marathon and founding the award-winning organization Empowered Women in Trades, is more than a story of individual resilience. It reflects a broader, pressing need for transformation in how we lead and operate within the rapidly evolving world of corporations, especially in male-dominated industries.

In navigating the uncharted waters of today's global changes, the lessons learned from my journey highlight the importance of adaptability, empathy, and a forward-thinking mindset. These tools will empower leaders to steer their organizations towards inclusivity and innovation, enabling both men and women to thrive equally. The demand for such transformational leadership has never been more acute as we strive to create workplaces that attract, retain, and elevate female talent, thereby enriching the tapestry of our organizational cultures with a diversity of thought, experience, and perspective.

Feminine and Masculine Psychology:
A Journey to Balance

Throughout my recovery, I was introduced to the concept of masculine and feminine psychology as a way to support my psychological strength in overcoming the hardest challenge of my life: learning to walk again. This framework offered a profound lens through which I could understand the emotional and mental resilience required to navigate such an immense journey.

Masculine psychology, with its emphasis on traits like determination, logic, and independence, aligned with the drive I needed to push through the physical pain and uncertainty. At the same time, feminine psychology, rooted in qualities like empathy, vulnerability, and intuition, provided the emotional support and self-compassion essential for healing. It was through embracing the balance and interplay between these two dimensions that I found the strength to confront my fears, harness my resilience, and rebuild my life step by step.

This introduction to the synergy of masculine and feminine traits helped me see how their overlap forms the foundation of our basic human psychological needs:

autonomy, competence, and belonging. By integrating these elements, I reclaimed my ability to walk and developed a deeper understanding of the psychological tools necessary to overcome life's most profound challenges.

This fascination became a guiding light in my journey of self-discovery, resilience, and leadership. Prior to the accident I operated in my masculine psychology had always been my default setting. From the dressage arena, where precision and control were everything, to the sports field where grit and competitiveness were praised, and into boardrooms and job sites dominated by men—I unconsciously anchored myself in my masculine psychology. Discipline, achievement, and relentless drive became my default, because everywhere I looked the world rewarded those qualities as the only currency of success. For a long time, I viewed my feminine traits—empathy, collaboration, and emotional intuition—as weaknesses to suppress.

However, the accident and its aftermath forced me to confront this imbalance head-on. My recovery required more than physical strength and determination, hallmarks of masculine energy, but also the vulnerability, self-compassion, and emotional resilience often linked to feminine psychology. In embracing and transitioning between these two dimensions, I found the key to true strength and holistic healing.

Psychologists like Carl Jung, who pioneered the

concept of anima and animus, offer profound insights into integrating masculine and feminine elements within each of us. Jung emphasized that wholeness arises when we embrace both aspects of our psyche, allowing them to coexist and complement one another. Similarly, contemporary scholars such as Susan David, who explores emotional agility, and Brené Brown, who highlights vulnerability's power, reinforce this integration's importance in achieving psychological health and leadership effectiveness.

In my recovery, I discovered that the overlap of masculine and feminine psychology aligns with our most basic human needs: autonomy, competence, and belonging, as defined by self-determination theory. Autonomy resonates with masculine traits of independence and self-direction, while belonging reflects the feminine need for connection and collaboration. Competence, the ability to master and grow, emerges as a synthesis of both.

By mastering the ability to transition between these psychological dimensions, I was able to adapt to the challenges of recovery and emerge stronger, more self-aware, and authentically aligned. In moments of physical pain and struggle, I leaned on my masculine drive to push through. In moments of emotional vulnerability, I allowed my feminine side to nurture and heal me. This balance became my greatest asset—not only in my recovery but in my leadership journey.

The lessons I learned through this process extend far beyond personal healing. Just as I found strength in integrating masculine and feminine psychology, organizations can achieve resilience and innovation by fostering cultures that value both dimensions. Leaders who harness the full spectrum of human psychology—strength and vulnerability, logic and intuition, can create environments where employees feel empowered to bring their whole selves to work.

The Dual Power of Masculine and Feminine Psychology in Leadership

Leadership in the modern workplace requires more than technical skills or strategic vision; it demands a deep understanding of human psychology and the ability to empower individuals while fostering psychological well-being. At the heart of this lies the dynamic interplay between masculine and feminine psychology—two complementary forces that exist within all of us. By learning to harness and balance these energies, leaders can create environments where people thrive and organizations flourish.

Understanding Masculine and Feminine Psychology

Masculine psychology as discussed, is often associated with traits such as assertiveness, independence, logic, and the drive to achieve. The energy propels us to set goals, take decisive action, and push through challenges. Feminine psychology, on the other hand, is rooted in empathy, collaboration, intuition, and nurturing. It is the energy that fosters connection, emotional intelligence, and adaptability.

While societal norms have historically positioned these traits as gender-specific, the reality is that every human possesses both masculine and feminine psychological traits. Leadership becomes truly transformative when we recognize that these energies are not oppositional but complementary. The key is learning when to lean into each energy based on the situation and the needs of the people you lead.

The Balancing Act: Knowing When to Lean Into Each Energy

Empowered leadership requires an acute awareness of when to utilize masculine energy and when to embrace feminine energy. For example:

- **Masculine Energy**: In moments of crisis or high-pressure decision-making, leaning into traits like assertiveness, focus, and resilience can help leaders cut through ambiguity and drive action. This energy is essential for creating clarity, setting direction, and maintaining uncertain stability.

- **Feminine Energy**: In conflict resolution, team building, or fostering innovation, embracing feminine traits like empathy, collaboration, and emotional intuition is crucial. This energy enables leaders to build trust, cultivate psychological safety, and unlock the collective creativity of their teams.

The most effective leaders understand that leaning exclusively into one energy creates an imbalance. Over-reliance on masculine energy can lead to rigidity, burnout, and a lack of connection. In contrast, overemphasizing feminine energy may result in indecisiveness or a reluctance to take bold action. True leadership involves mastering the ability to transition seamlessly between these energies, responding to the moment's needs with authenticity and intentionality.

Creating a Culture of Empowerment and Well-being

When leaders embrace both masculine and feminine psychology, they create a culture that empowers individuals and prioritizes psychological well-being. Here's how this balanced approach translates into actionable leadership practices:

1. **Empowering Autonomy**: Masculine energy can help establish clear expectations and provide the structure employees need to take ownership of their work. Feminine energy ensures that this autonomy is supported by empathy, understanding, and resources.

2. **Fostering Collaboration**: Feminine energy enables leaders to create inclusive environments where diverse perspectives are valued. This builds a sense of belonging and psychological safety, encouraging employees to share ideas and innovate. Masculine energy drives these ideas forward, turning collaboration into actionable outcomes.

3. **Adapting to Change**: The workplace is ever-evolving, and leaders must be adaptable. Feminine energy fosters openness to new ideas and emotional resilience, while masculine energy provides the focus and determination to implement change effectively.

4. **Leading with Emotional Intelligence**: Emotional intelligence bridges masculine and feminine psychology. Leaders with high emotional intelligence understand their own emotions and those of others, leveraging this awareness to make thoughtful decisions and inspire their teams.

To become a leader who empowers humans and fosters high psychological well-being levels, you must start with self-awareness. Reflect on your natural tendencies—do you lean more heavily into masculine or feminine energy?

How does this affect your leadership style and the culture of your organization? From this awareness foundation, begin to develop the agility to balance both energies. Cultivate empathy alongside assertiveness, logic alongside intuition, and independence alongside collaboration. Recognize that leadership is not about embodying one archetype but about integrating the strengths of both masculine and feminine psychology to lead authentically and effectively.

As leaders, we hold the power to transform our workplaces into environments where people can bring their whole selves to work, feel valued, and contribute meaningfully. By embracing the duality of masculine and feminine psychology, we can create cultures that achieve high performance and prioritize every individual's well-being and humanity. In doing so, we redefine what it means to lead in the modern workplace, paving the way for a more inclusive, compassionate, and resilient future.

This book is more than a recount of personal triumph over adversity; it is a clarion call for a seismic shift in our leadership paradigms and organizational cultures. By exploring how the integration of key principles can address the *Billion Dollar Blind Spot*, we uncover pathways to foster psychological well-being, inclusivity, and shared humanity in our organizations.

Rooted in our fundamental psychological needs—autonomy, competence, and belonging—this approach aims to create workplaces that are not only productive but also deeply fulfilling. It is a guide for navigating the complexities of the modern workplace, armed with the conviction that the opportunity for profound growth and transformation lies through adversity.

As we turn the page to the next chapter, let us carry forward the lessons of resilience, adaptability, and unwavering commitment to fostering environments where every individual has the opportunity to excel and contribute to their fullest potential. By embracing these principles, we can redefine leadership and organizational culture, creating a future where all voices are valued and every person thrives.

Masculinity is Being Questioned

Being male is a matter of birth.
Being a man is a matter of choice
—Edwin Louis Cole

Gender norms and stereotypes are powerful forces that shape attitudes and behaviors from a young age, influencing how individuals view themselves and others. These norms are societal constructs that define what is considered "appropriate" for men and women, dictating behaviors, roles, and expectations. Unlike personal beliefs and actions, which are shaped by individual experiences and values, gender norms operate on a collective level, reinforcing stereotypes that perpetuate inequality.

For instance, traditional gender norms often portray men as stoic, dominant, and providers, while women are expected to be nurturing, emotional, and caretakers. These broad generalizations limit both genders, creating a continuous cycle of stereotyping. Boys and men, for example, may feel pressured to suppress vulnerability and conform to ideals of strength and toughness. In contrast, girls and women may feel constrained by expectations to prioritize others over themselves.

This cycle is self-reinforcing. When individuals act following these stereotypes, they perpetuate the norms, creating environments where deviation is discouraged. Over time, these norms become embedded in organizational cultures, shaping hiring decisions, leadership styles, and workplace dynamics.

The Impact of Gender Norms on Men and Women

For men, these stereotypes often result in emotional suppression, isolation, and a lack of connection to their authentic selves. They are taught to "man up," masking struggles that could otherwise be addressed through open dialogue and support. This limits their ability to embrace emotional intelligence, collaborate effectively, and lead with authenticity.

For women, these norms can create barriers to entry and advancement in traditionally male-dominated fields. They may face scrutiny or resistance when stepping into leadership roles, as their assertiveness is often misinterpreted through the lens of gender bias. This perpetuates a lack of representation at decision-making levels and hinders organizations from reaping the benefits of diverse leadership.

I experienced this firsthand during a high-stakes meeting where I was the only woman in the room. The discussion had become increasingly heated, with one of the male participants aggressively berating the team, his assertiveness seemingly accepted without question. As the tension escalated and the conversation veered into unproductive territory, I decided enough was enough. I intervened with a strong and assertive voice, making it clear that the behavior was counterproductive and that we needed to refocus on solutions rather than blame.

What followed was eye-opening. Instead of being acknowledged for bringing the conversation back on track, I was accused of "yelling" and behaving inappropriately. My assertiveness—a trait often celebrated in male leaders—was perceived as confrontational and out of place. The very same behavior that had been tolerated, even respected, in my male counterpart was met with criticism when displayed by me.

This moment underscored the deeply ingrained gender norms that shape expectations around leadership behavior. While a man's assertiveness was seen as a strength, mine was viewed through the lens of stereotypes that expect women to be more conciliatory and less forceful. It wasn't about what was said but about who said it, a reflection of the subtle yet pervasive bias that limits women from being fully accepted as equals in leadership roles.

These experiences highlight the urgent need to challenge and dismantle these norms, creating workplace cultures where behavior is assessed based on merit and impact rather than outdated expectations tied to gender. This is more than just addressing the bias women face when displaying traditionally masculine traits; it's also about liberating men from the cages of silence imposed by these same gender norms.

In the situation described, the other men in the room believed that showing respect to their leader meant silently enduring inappropriate treatment, even if it conflicted with their values or the need for a healthier workplace dynamic. Gender norms dictated their response, stifling their ability to speak up and advocate for respect—not only for themselves but for everyone in the room. This highlights the broader issue: these norms harm us all by perpetuating environments where respect and dignity are conditional rather than funda-mental rights.

Respect equality is not about shifting power dynamics to favor one group over another; it is about ensuring that all individuals, regardless of gender, are treated with the respect and dignity they inherently deserve as human beings. By dismantling these outdated constructs, we can create inclusive workplace cultures that empower everyone to lead, collaborate, and contribute authentically. Only then can we truly unlock the potential of diverse leadership and foster environments where every human has the opportunity to thrive.

Breaking the Cycle

To break the cycle of gender stereotyping, organizations must actively challenge these norms and foster environments where individuality is celebrated. This involves:

1. **Raising Awareness**: Educate employees about the influence of gender norms and stereotypes, helping them understand how these societal constructs shape attitudes and behaviors.
2. **Encouraging Authenticity**: Promote a workplace culture that values diverse expressions of masculinity and femininity, allowing individuals to lead in ways that align with their authentic selves.
3. **Implementing Inclusive Policies**: Create structures that counteract the effects of gender norms, such as mentorship programs for underrepresented groups, policies supporting emotional well-being, and training focused on unconscious bias.

By addressing these norms and their impact, organizations can create a more inclusive culture that empowers everyone, regardless of gender, to thrive. This approach benefits individuals and strengthens organizational performance by leveraging the full potential of a diverse workforce.

This book is a call to reimagine how we approach gender in the workplace. Gender norms and stereotypes may seem intangible, but their impact is concrete, shaping behaviors, limiting potential, and perpetuating inequalities. To truly embrace diversity and inclusion, we must dismantle these norms, replace them with values of respect and empathy, and create spaces where all individuals feel empowered to lead, collaborate, and innovate.

By recognizing and challenging the influence of gender norms, we can break free from the limitations they impose and build workplaces that celebrate the full spectrum of human potential. This transformation is not just about achieving equity—it's about unlocking the strength and resilience that come from diversity, creating a brighter future for everyone.

Rethinking Diversity and Inclusion Programs

While well-intentioned, traditional diversity and inclusion programs can inadvertently create feelings of shame and defensiveness among men. Research highlights how these initiatives often highlight systemic imbalances and unconscious biases, which, while critical to address, can leave some men feeling singled out or blamed for issues rooted in broader societal structures. This can lead to questioning their masculinity and their place in the evolving workplace.

Studies such as those by Ely and Meyerson, demonstrate that traditional diversity initiatives can sometimes backfire by reinforcing an "us versus them" mentality. Men, particularly those in leadership roles, may feel their contributions are undervalued or that they are being asked to abdicate their role in the workplace hierarchy. When men feel shamed or excluded from the conversation, the result is often disengagement rather than the allyship necessary for fostering genuine inclusivity.

For example, a diversity workshop might unintentionally frame men as inherently privileged or resistant to change without considering the nuanced experiences and struggles they face, such as societal pressures to conform to rigid masculine norms. This approach can make men reluctant to engage in these conversations, perceiving them as attacks on their identity rather than opportunities for growth and collaboration.

To create truly inclusive workplaces, we must shift the focus from the differences that divide us—like gender—to fostering environments where respect, equality, and psychological safety thrive. This means reframing diversity and inclusion programs to highlight the value of collaboration, mutual learning, and each individual's unique strengths.

Instead of focusing solely on historical inequities, organizations should emphasize the concept of *respect equality*—the belief that everyone, regardless of gender or background, deserves equal respect and opportunities. This approach fosters an environment where people can learn from one another, appreciating and integrating the strengths of those different from themselves.

Imagine the power of applying the principle of 1 + 1 = 3. When we combine our strengths with those of others, we create something far greater than the sum of its parts. A man's decisiveness and strategic thinking, paired with a woman's empathy and intuition, can lead to innovative solutions and stronger leadership. When we move beyond focusing on gender as a dividing line and instead embrace it as one of many dimensions of human diversity, we unlock a world of possibility.

What Needs to Change

To make this shift, organizations must:

1. **Redesign Diversity Training**: Move away from programs that highlight blame or division. Instead, focus on

cultivating curiosity about others' experiences, fostering empathy, and building skills for effective collaboration.

2. **Promote Psychological Safety**: Ensure that all individuals—men included—feel safe to share their thoughts and emotions without fear of judgment or exclusion. This includes normalizing conversations about vulnerability and emotional intelligence as strengths.

3. **Celebrate Strengths in Diversity**: Highlight how differences complement and amplify strengths rather than serving as sources of division. Create opportunities for employees to learn from one another's perspectives, skills, and approaches.

4. **Engage Men as Allies**: Actively involve men in diversity and inclusion efforts, not as bystanders or adversaries but as integral partners in creating inclusive workplaces. Frame these initiatives as opportunities to lead with greater authenticity and impact.

By fostering a culture prioritizing respect, equality, and psychological safety, we can transform workplaces into environments where everyone—regardless of gender—feels valued, empowered, and inspired to contribute. This shift is essential for addressing the *Billion Dollar Blind Spot* and creating a future where our collective strengths build something truly extraordinary. It's time to move beyond programs that divide us and embrace the transformative power of unity, respect, and mutual growth. Together, we can create organizations that reflect the best of humanity and the boundless potential of collaboration.

Redefining Masculinity in the Workplace

We find ourselves at the crossroads of two pivotal shifts reshaping the contemporary workplace: the rise of artificial intelligence and the push for diversity and inclusion. These revolutions are prompting a revaluation of traditional notions of masculinity, particularly the foundational principles of appreciation and respect. However, amidst the drive for diverse and inclusive initiatives, we have inadvertently overlooked the importance of inclusivity for men in the workplace. In our quest to create inclusive environments, we have strayed from the essence of true inclusivity and belonging, which demands that all individuals feel valued and respected. The result is a significant proportion of people feeling unsafe to speak up. In pushing so hard for diversity, often with an aggressive "it is our time" undertone, we have inadvertently created an environment where some individuals feel victimized and silenced.

This is the exact opposite of what true inclusivity and belonging is about. Inclusivity is not about replacing one dominant group with another; it is about creating a culture where everyone feels empowered and respected regardless of their background or identity. To achieve genuine inclusivity, we must ensure that our efforts do not alienate or marginalize any group, including men, but rather foster an environment where all voices are heard and valued. Achieving genuine inclusivity means recognizing and addressing the unique experiences and challenges faced by all in our workplaces.

To bridge this gap, we must cultivate workplace cultures that both empower minority groups whilst also honoring the diverse expression of healthy masculinity; this entails recognizing and celebrating the unique contributions and expressions of men in the workplace, thereby fostering an environment where all individuals, regardless of gender or background, feel a sense of belonging and inclusion. In an AI-driven world, workplaces must actively consider how to empower humans by redefining masculinity and embracing diverse strengths. This approach not only fosters psychological safety but also ensures that organizations leverage the full potential of their people, creating cultures where innovation and inclusivity thrive together.

In subsequent chapters of this book, we delve deeper into the complexities of masculinity and explore the effects of society's patriarchal system on men's well-being. Through analysis and reflection, we aim to shed light on the multifaceted nature of masculinity in the modern workplace and pave the way for more inclusive and supportive organizational cultures. Masculine strengths, such as resilience, protection, and decisive action, are vital in building inclusive workplaces and fostering psychological safety. Men play an essential role in this journey, contributing unique perspectives and leadership qualities that empower organizations to achieve high psychological well-being and inclusivity for all.

Navigating the complexities of masculinity in the contemporary workplace reveals a compelling narrative that often goes untold—one shaped by evolving societal expectations, entrenched gender norms, and the pressures of modern organizational culture. Traditionally associated with traits such as stoicism, dominance, and assertiveness, masculinity is being redefined in response to the increasing demand for inclusivity, emotional intelligence, and collaborative leadership. This shift, while necessary, has created a unique set of challenges for men as they grapple with the tension between traditional ideals and contemporary workplace dynamics.

Through the lens of research by Paludi and Bauer (2019) and Kimmel (2019), we examine men's lived experiences navigating these shifting paradigms. Paludi and Bauer highlight how traditional definitions of masculinity, often reinforced by patriarchal structures, can create environments where men feel compelled to suppress emotions and conform to outdated norms. These pressures limit men's ability to connect authentically with others and stifle their potential to contribute meaningfully to diverse and inclusive organizational cultures.

Kimmel's research further explores the intersection of societal expectations and professional realities, shedding light on how power dynamics and gendered expectations shape men's experiences in the workplace. Men are often caught in a paradox: they are encouraged to demonstrate strength and authority while simultaneously being asked to embody traits like vulnerability and empathy, which are increasingly valued in leadership. This dichotomy can lead to confusion, resistance, and a sense of inadequacy as they navigate these conflicting demands.

These studies reveal that men's challenges are not merely individual struggles, but systemic issues deeply embedded in organizational cultures. The negative narratives men in today's workplaces underscore the urgent need for a broader dialogue on how masculinity is understood and expressed. By addressing these complexities, organizations can create environments that honor the diverse expressions of masculinity, empowering men to lead authentically while contributing to inclusive and supportive workplace cultures.

Ultimately, men's lived experiences in professional

settings illuminate the need for organizations to challenge outdated gender norms actively. By fostering cultures that embrace both traditional and evolving expressions of masculinity, workplaces can unlock the potential of all individuals, ensuring that men are not only included in the diversity and inclusion journey but also positioned as allies and champions of positive organizational change. This approach is essential for creating psychologically safe workplaces where everyone, regardless of gender, can thrive.

Imagine John, an upper-level manager in a bustling corporate office. John embodies many of the traits traditionally associated with masculinity, such as strength, stoicism, and assertiveness, which, to date, have been rewarded by society and organizations. Nevertheless, beneath this facade lies a complex inner world, shaped by the changing societal expectations and workplace dynamics, driving John to navigate his leadership in silence while grappling with conflicting messages about what it means to be a man in the modern workplace. As a leader, he is being asked to create psychologically safe workplaces that foster high levels of inclusivity; however, when he doesn't feel safe to speak up, ask questions or show emotion, how can we ask him to lead a culture that creates this for others?

Paludi and Bauer's research highlights the tension between traditional masculinity and the evolving needs of modern workplaces. Traditional norms, emphasizing dominance and stoicism, often conflict with the collaborative and emotionally intelligent leadership styles that today's organizations require. This misalignment fosters disengagement, stifles innovation, and perpetuates toxic cultures that drive talent away.

The cost of these issues is significant. Studies show that poor organizational cultures lead to low employee engagement, reduced productivity, and high turnover, collectively costing businesses billions annually. Deloitte reports that turnover and lost productivity due to disengagement can cost a company up to 34% of an employee's annual salary. In addition, the World Health Organization estimates that depression and anxiety—exacerbated by poor workplace environments—cost the global economy $1 trillion annually in lost productivity.

Adapting to a more inclusive definition of masculinity—one that values empathy, collaboration, and emotional intelligence—can address these challenges. Inclusive workplaces are better for employee well-being and drive financial success. For example, Boston Consulting Group found that companies with above-average diversity on management teams report innovation revenue 19% higher than their less diverse counterparts.

Creating psychologically safe cultures that embrace diverse expressions of masculinity is critical to reversing these losses. When employees feel valued and safe to express their authentic selves, organizations unlock their full potential, resulting in stronger team cohesion, better decision-making, and a more competitive edge in today's market. Addressing these cultural deficits is not just a step toward equity—it's a business imperative.

Similarly, Kimmel's work delves into the complexity of American masculinity, exploring how societal shifts and power dynamics shape men's experiences in the workplace. Through his research, we gain a deeper understanding of men's pressures and constraints as they navigate the intersection of gender power and identity in professional settings. Together, these studies paint a nuanced portrait of masculinity in the modern workplace, challenging us to reconsider our assumptions and biases towards men. By acknowledging men's diverse experiences and perspectives, organizations can create more inclusive and supportive cultures that empower all individuals to thrive.

As organizations strive to foster more diverse and inclusive workplaces, it's crucial to examine the impact of these initiatives on the male experience. Swim et al.'s (2019) research reveals the complexities surrounding traditional diversity training programs and the implications for men in professional settings. Traditional diversity training programs are often designed to raise awareness of unconscious bias, promote inclusive behaviors and mitigate discrimination in the workplace. However, Swim's research suggests these programs may not always address the root cause of bias or foster genuine cultural change.

One of the critical shortcomings of traditional diversity training lies in its tendency to skim the surface, merely scratching at the underlying issues of bias and inequality. Rather than fostering a genuine understanding of diverse experiences and encouraging inclusive behaviors, these programs often focus on compliance and awareness without offering actionable strategies for meaningful change. This superficial approach can inadvertently alienate certain groups, particularly men, by framing them as the problem rather than part of the solution.

During an interview, a male participant shared his feelings after completing a compulsory diversity training program:

"After the training, I felt like I was being told that just being born male made me what's wrong with the world. As a middle-aged white man, I walked away thinking my opinion no longer mattered, that my time was over, and I should just stay silent."

This outcome underscores a significant flaw in the approach of many traditional diversity training programs. Rather than fostering inclusion, it left this individual feeling excluded, undervalued, and voiceless—a stark contradiction to the very principles of diversity and inclusion these initiatives aim to promote.

The result is not empowerment but disengagement, where men may feel alienated and hesitant to contribute. This is a failure of diversity and inclusion, which should aim to create environments where all individuals, regardless of gender, background, or identity, feel respected and valued.

Diversity and inclusion include men. The purpose is not to replace one group's dominance with another but to foster a collaborative environment where all voices matter, and everyone's strengths are recognized and utilized. The focus must shift from assigning blame to building bridges, emphasizing mutual respect and understanding. As this example illustrates, diversity initiatives that fail to embrace men as allies and partners risk deepening divides rather than bridging them, undermining the critical goal of creating workplaces where everyone can thrive.

Addressing this issue requires redesigning diversity training programs to include actionable steps for allyship, open dialogue, and collaborative problem-solving. We can only begin to dismantle the biases and stereotypes that hold workplaces back by fostering an inclusive definition of diversity that empowers all participants. Inclusivity is not about silencing voices; it's about ensuring everyone's voice has the space to contribute to progress.

While these traditional programs may shed light on unconscious biases, they often fall short in providing actionable strategies for confronting and dismantling these biases in real-world scenarios. Furthermore, as Swim emphasizes, traditional diversity training initiatives may unintentionally reinforce microaggressions and perpetuate organizational power imbalances. By compartmentalizing diversity and inclusion as standalone topics, rather than intrinsic elements of organizational culture, these programs inadvertently convey to men that their experiences and viewpoints are of lesser importance compared to those of minority groups.

Furthermore, traditional diversity training programs often lack meaningful engagement and follow-up mechanisms to ensure lasting behavioral change. Without ongoing support and accountability, participants may struggle to translate their newfound awareness into tangible actions and organizational change. Organizations must adopt a more holistic and inclusive approach to diversity and inclusion initiatives to address these limitations.

This involves moving beyond one-off training sessions and integrating diversity and inclusion principles into all aspects of organizational culture, policies, and practices. By fostering open dialogue, promoting allyship, and creating opportunities for genuine engagement and collaboration among all organization members, workplaces can enable men to discover a new, empowered definition of masculinity that supports their psychological well-being and those around them. This approach ensures men feel valued, respected, and included; it also positions them as active contributors to a broader diversity and inclusion agenda, fostering environments where everyone can thrive.

Swim's research underscores the importance of critically evaluating the effectiveness of diversity training programs and adopting a more comprehensive approach to fostering diversity and inclusion in the workplace by challenging entrenched biases and power dynamics. By integrating the principles of positive psychology—such as focusing on strengths, fostering gratitude, and cultivating empathy—organizations can shift from surface-level interventions to meaningful cultural transformation. This approach emphasizes creating environments where all individuals, including men, feel a genuine sense of belonging and inclusion. Positive psychology provides tools to build resilience, enhance interpersonal relationships, and promote psychological safety, ensuring diversity efforts empower all employees and lead to sustainable organizational success.

In our current organizational landscape, there's a silent revolution brewing where men's hearts and minds grapple with the very essence of masculinity and their place in the world. As we strive for diversity and inclusion within our organizations, we often overlook men's critical role in achieving this, failing to appreciate and respect their contributions fully. This oversight undermines the well-being of men and poses a significant threat to organizational productivity, employee engagement, and overall success.

The Essential Role of Belonging

A core goal of any inclusive effort should be to create a sense of belonging for all individuals. Belonging is a fundamental human need deeply rooted in feminine psychology, emphasizing community, connection, and mutual care. When employees feel a genuine sense of belonging at work, they are more engaged, motivated, and collaborative, fostering a culture of innovation and trust. Conversely, the absence of belonging can lead to disengagement, increased stress, and a lack of psychological safety. Employees who feel alienated or undervalued may withdraw, leading to lower productivity, higher turnover, and a toxic work environment that impacts organizational performance.

The Cost of Not Belonging

When people do not feel a sense of belonging, it affects both individuals and the broader organization. On an individual level, it can result in feelings of isolation, lowered self-esteem, and even mental health challenges such as anxiety and depression. At the organizational level, the lack of belonging leads to reduced employee retention, poor collaboration, and diminished morale. According to research, employees who do not feel included are less likely to go above and beyond in their roles and are more likely to leave their positions, costing organizations both talent and financial resources.

Leveraging Masculine and Feminine Psychology

To address this, organizations must harness both masculine and feminine psychological strengths. Masculine psychology, with its emphasis on protection and structure, can play a pivotal role in creating environments where employees feel emotionally and physically safe. When leaders adopt a protective mindset, they foster trust and establish boundaries that shield employees from harmful behaviors, such as discrimination or harassment. This sense of safety is a prerequisite for fostering belonging.

On the other hand, feminine psychology, which centers on community and nurturing relationships, is vital for cultivating genuine connection and inclusivity. Organizations can create a culture where diverse voices are heard, respected, and valued by prioritizing empathy, collaboration, and open dialogue. Combining these two approaches—protection and community—creates a powerful synergy that fosters prosocial behavior and psychological well-being.

The Power of Prosocial Behavior

When organizations integrate masculine and feminine psychological principles, they encourage prosocial behaviors—actions that benefit others and contribute to a positive social environment. These behaviors, such as collaboration, mutual support, and active listening, enhance workplace relationships and drive collective success. A workplace that balances protection with community is one where employees feel empowered to contribute their best selves, knowing they are valued and supported.

Building the Foundation

To achieve this balance, leaders must:

1. **Promote Psychological Safety:** Establish clear policies and behaviors that protect employees from harm and encourage open, honest communication.
2. **Foster Connection:** Create spaces where individuals can share their experiences, build relationships, and find common ground, reinforcing a sense of community.
3. **Model Inclusive Leadership:** Demonstrate both protective and nurturing behaviors, showing that leadership involves strength, empathy, and a commitment to fairness.

4. **Encourage Collaborative Solutions:** Involve employees in diversity and inclusion efforts, ensuring everyone has a voice in creating an environment that works for all.

Empowering Men and Enriching Organizations

By integrating the principles discussed, organizations can redefine their approach to diversity and inclusion. Cultures that honor the strengths of both masculine and feminine psychology ensure all employees feel a sense of belonging and purpose. This not only addresses the well-being of men but also elevates the collective psychological well-being of the organization, paving the way for sustainable success.

Traditional ideals of strength, stoicism, and dominance have long boxed men into a narrow definition of masculinity, creating a toxic environment where vulnerability is shunned, emotions are suppressed, and authentic human connections are hindered. These restrictive norms leave many men questioning their identities and struggling to reconcile societal expectations with their true selves. When men are denied the freedom to express their full humanity, their innovation, collaboration, and leadership potential is stifled, leading to diminished organizational performance and disengagement.

Neglecting to address these unique challenges perpetuates a cycle of silence and isolation, exacerbating mental health issues and leaving men grappling with feelings of inadequacy and disconnection. These outcomes harm individuals and ripple across organizations, contributing to the *Billion Dollar Blind Spot.*

It's time for organizations to actively support the psychological well-being of men by creating inclusive cultures that celebrate the diversity of masculine experiences. Positive masculine traits—such as empathy, collaboration, and a protective instinct—are invaluable in fostering respect and psychological safety within teams. Combined with feminine psychology's communal strengths, these traits drive prosocial behavior and help build cohesive, high-performing environments.

Together, we can empower men to thrive personally and professionally by acknowledging, appreciating, and respecting their experiences. This is not about giving men more power but enabling them to connect with the human condition and contribute authentically. By championing their voices and embracing their strength, we can pave the way for workplaces where all individuals, regardless of gender, can flourish.

This book is a call to action for organizations to create spaces where men and women work collaboratively to foster diversity, inclusion, and belonging. Let's make men allies, champions, and heroes of this journey and shape a future where psychological safety and respect equality are foundational pillars. Together, we can create a brighter future for everyone, turning the vision of truly inclusive workplaces into reality.

Let's make men the allies, champions and heroes of our diversity and inclusion journey and create a brighter future for everyone.

Pin the Tail on the CEO

Manage for culture, not revenue.
—Adam Coffey

In the high-stakes business world, the CEO often serves as the one person we want to "pin the tail" on; the primary focal point for both praise and blame when it comes to organizational performance. However, the notion of "pinning the tail on the CEO" oversimplifies the complex dynamics at play within an organization, particularly when it comes to fostering strong workplace cultures. While CEOs undoubtedly play a crucial role in setting the tone and direction of a company, the responsibility for shaping organizational culture and fostering a sense of belonging and inclusion extends far beyond the corner office with the best view.

Ironically, amidst the laser focus of CEOs and executives on building revenue to meet shareholders' expectations or chasing that big exit, organizational culture is often overlooked, leading to substantial financial losses for businesses globally. Research has shown that poor workplace culture costs companies billions in lost productivity, increased turnover, and healthcare expenses. This underscores the critical importance of prioritizing positive organizational culture alongside revenue and short-term gains.

I want to challenge the conventional wisdom that places the burden of culture solely on the shoulders of top executives and instead, advocate for a more holistic approach to leadership and culture management. Drawing inspiration from Adam Coffey's perspective, we explore the idea that many CEOs and entrepreneurs are primarily focused on revenue, a natural inclination given the competitive nature of the business world. However, Coffey's teaching in his book 'Empire Builder' reminds us that prioritizing revenue over culture is not only shortsighted, it is ultimately counterproductive.

According to Coffey, true business success cannot be achieved through top-down revenue management alone, and he would know, as he has masterfully navigated the business landscape, achieving over $2.5 billion in exits. Instead, it requires a concerted effort to build a strong organizational culture from the ground up that values diversity, inclusion, and employee well-being. Organizations can create a more resilient, adaptable, sustainable and high-performing workforce by empowering leaders at all levels to prioritize culture over revenue and short-term gains.

Coffey's philosophy of 'manage for culture, not revenue' challenges traditional notions of corporate leadership by emphasizing the importance of prioritizing organizational culture over immediate financial gains. This approach underscores the idea that a thriving culture serves as the bedrock for long-term success and sustainability, with tangible impacts on profits and EBITDA.

Research consistently demonstrates that inclusivity and gender respect are both moral imperatives and strategic advantages. For example, McKinsey's studies reveal that organizations with diverse executive teams are 25% more likely to outperform their peers in profitability, and those fostering inclusive environments see higher employee engagement and retention rates—key drivers of operational efficiency and financial performance. These factors directly contribute to improved EBITDA by reducing turnover costs, enhancing productivity, and fostering innovation through diverse perspectives.

By focusing on building a positive and inclusive culture, CEOs and leaders create environments where employees feel valued, respected, and empowered to bring their full selves to work. This drives engagement and unlocks creativity and collaboration, critical components of sustained revenue growth. When inclusivity is woven into the organizational fabric, it leads to higher employee satisfaction, which correlates with improved customer satisfaction—another vital contributor to profitability.

Coffey's philosophy aligns with this evidence, challenging leaders to shift their focus from short-term revenue targets to cultivating cultures that prioritize psychological safety and gender respect. This strategic shift transforms inclusivity and respect into financial assets, ensuring that the organization is ethical and positioned for robust financial health and competitive advantage.

The conversation around organizational culture must address the silencing effects of traditional masculine norms, particularly on men in leadership roles. For generations, men have been socialized to suppress emotions and adopt a stoic facade, often equating vulnerability with weakness. While this conditioning might have once been seen as a strength in leadership, it now hinders their ability to foster inclusive and supportive workplace cultures. These outdated norms can prevent leaders from building authentic connections, stifling their capacity to lead with empathy and innovation.

Leaders must challenge these deeply ingrained norms to create a genuine sense of belonging and promote diversity. Embracing vulnerability is not a sign of weakness but a demonstration of courage and emotional intelligence. By acknowledging their limitations and biases, leaders can open the door to more meaningful understanding of their teams' diverse experiences and perspectives. This shift enhances psychological safety and empowers leaders to build cultures that thrive on collaboration, respect, and shared purpose.

For organizations to succeed in today's complex, fast-evolving landscape, leaders must transcend traditional notions of stoicism and embrace the transformative power of empathy and connection. Through this evolution, they can create environments where all individuals feel valued, supported, and inspired to contribute their best.

In essence, Coffey's philosophy serves as a rallying call for CEOs and leaders to prioritize the human aspect of business, recognizing that cultivating a positive culture is as morally imperative as strategically advantageous. By embracing empathy, vulnerability, and a commitment to inclusivity, leaders can lay the groundwork for organizations that thrive on diversity, innovation, and collective success.

So why do we want to pin the tail on the CEOs when fostering organizational culture?

Subcultures:
The Puzzle Pieces of Organizational Culture

While CEOs play a pivotal role in shaping the overarching organizational culture, the reality of any business is that it comprises various subcultures within individual teams or departments. These subcultures are like puzzle pieces that form the complete picture of organizational culture. Each team contributes unique values, dynamics, and approaches, creating a mosaic reflecting the broader company ethos.

For instance, the culture of a sales team often reflects the traits of risk-taking, ambition, and a relentless drive to "hunt the sale." This team thrives on pushing boundaries, embracing uncertainty, and celebrating wins. On the other hand, a finance team typically embodies values of precision, caution, and analytical rigor, operating as the steady hand that "keeps the score" and ensures the organization remains grounded in sound decision-making. While aligned under the same organizational vision and values, these two teams can have distinctly different cultures catering to their unique roles and priorities.

CEOs' challenge—and opportunity—is ensuring these diverse subcultures are cohesively linked to the overarching organizational culture. While individual teams may operate differently, their values must ultimately align with the company's mission and strategic goals. CEOs must act as the glue that binds these subcultures together, fostering mutual respect and collaboration across departments. This involves promoting open communication, recognizing the unique strengths of each team, and ensuring alignment to the company's core values.

CEOs can create an environment where teams thrive individually and collectively by acknowledging and respecting the differences between subcultures while cultivating a shared sense of purpose and belonging. This harmony between subcultures drives high performance and reinforces a unified organizational culture that supports the company's long-term vision.

Co-Design:
Aligning Subcultures to Build the Bigger Picture

In today's complex and rapidly evolving business landscape, expecting CEOs to drive cultural transformation single-handedly is neither practical nor effective. The co-design approach offers a compelling solution, empowering leaders to collaboratively shape organizational culture while addressing the unique dynamics of team subcultures. This method provides a powerful way to connect the puzzle pieces of subcultures into a cohesive whole, ensuring that the overarching culture reflects the diversity and strengths of every team.

Subcultures, like the ambitious sales and the meticulous

finance teams, often operate with different priorities and approaches, as discussed earlier. CEOs can actively engage these distinct teams in defining and aligning cultural values through co-design. For instance, a co-design initiative might involve workshops where sales, finance, and other teams contribute their perspectives on what inclusion, collaboration, and innovation mean within their contexts. By bringing these voices together, the CEO fosters a sense of ownership among employees, ensuring the cultural framework resonates across all subcultures.

This collaborative approach transforms the CEO's role from a top-down enforcer of culture into a facilitator of connection. By leveraging the collective insights and experiences of their workforce, leaders can create a culture that reflects the organization's mission and vision and integrates each team's unique dynamics. This alignment ensures that individual subcultures maintain their distinct identities and strengths and contribute to and reinforce the larger organizational culture.

Co-design also addresses the critical issue of engagement. When employees feel heard and see their input shaping the company's culture, their sense of belonging and commitment deepens. This directly links to improved psychological well-being and enhanced collaboration across departments, fostering a culture of mutual respect and shared purpose.

By adopting co-design as a tool, CEOs can bridge the gaps between subcultures, creating a unified and inclusive organizational culture. This collaborative strategy ensures that every puzzle piece connects seamlessly, building a bigger picture where all teams thrive together while remaining true to their unique roles and contributions.

Let's explore how co-design can transform these critical areas of organizational culture.

1. **Set the Vision and Values:** In a co-design process for setting the vision and values, CEOs can initiate a collaborative effort that involves key stakeholders from across the organization, ranging from entry-level employees to top executives. By welcoming input and feedback from individuals at all levels of the hierarchy, CEOs ensure that the resulting vision and values truly reflect the collective aspirations and perspectives of the entire workforce. This inclusive approach strengthens buy-in and commitment and fosters a sense of ownership and alignment with the organizational culture.

   When employees see that their voices are heard and valued in shaping the company's direction, they are likelier to feel a sense of belonging and purpose, knowing that they are integral in driving the organization's success. CEOs create a culture of inclusivity, collaboration, and shared responsibility by putting everyone on equal footing in the co-design process, laying the groundwork for a thriving and resilient organization.

2. **Modelling Desired Behaviors:** A mistake some leaders make is that they stop at setting their organization's values and don't dig deeper into establishing the desired behaviors of those in the organization. To ensure that desired behaviors are modelled throughout the organization, the first step is to establish these behaviors in alignment with the company's values and culture. This process involves identifying the behaviors that good leadership exemplifies whilst gathering input from employees to determine the behaviors they want to see within the organization. This collaborative approach ensures that the promoted behaviors resonate with the entire workforce and reflect diverse perspectives.

    Rather than relying solely on the CEO to model these desired behaviors, organizations can implement leadership development programs that empower leaders at all levels to embody and uphold the organization's values and desired behaviors. Companies enable leaders to integrate these behaviors into their daily interactions and decision-making processes through training, coaching, and ongoing support. Additionally, CEOS must empower their leaders to perpetuate these behaviors within their teams, especially when onboarding new employees. By decentralizing the responsibility for modelling desired behaviors, companies create a culture where inclusivity, integrity, and accountability are upheld by all organization members, fostering a sense of belonging and cohesion across teams. This ongoing process of reinforcement and empowerment ensures that the organization's culture remains dynamic and responsive to its workforce's evolving needs and expectations.

3. **Promoting Diversity and Inclusion:** CEOs and leaders must first embark on a journey of self-reflection to understand how they experience a sense of belonging in the workplace. By uncovering their own sources of belonging, leaders can better support their teams in cultivating a culture of inclusivity. This entails creating an environment where vulnerability is welcomed, and leaders feel comfortable admitting their uncertainties about fostering inclusivity because we all have them.

   From a foundation of vulnerability, a place of true strength, leaders of all levels can engage in a collaborative co-design process, embracing a mindset of appreciation for differences and a willingness to learn from one another. Through this process, teams can collectively explore how to support each individual's sense of belonging, particularly those from diverse backgrounds. Education and training initiatives can equip team members with the tools and knowledge to understand and embrace diversity, fostering an environment where everyone feels valued and respected. By fostering a culture of inclusivity from the ground up, CEOs and leaders empower their teams to create workplaces where every voice is heard and everyone feels a sense of belonging.

4. **Prioritizing Employee Well-being:** Employee well-being extends beyond surface-level inclusivity initiatives; it requires a profound cultural shift that creates an environment where individuals from all backgrounds can thrive, including those shaped by traditional masculine norms. These norms, often characterized by emotional suppression and unyielding self-reliance, can significantly harm mental health, particularly for men. Research from the *Journal of Counselling Psychology* establishes a direct link between adherence to these norms and poor mental health outcomes. At the same time, findings from the *American Psychological Association* reveal that leaders conforming to these ideologies are less likely to foster open communication, weakening the critical support systems needed for well-being.

    This traditional "command and control" leadership

style has further implications. As the Harvard Business Review highlighted, such approaches often suppress creativity and engagement within teams, creating a work environment that stifles innovation. Conversely, leaders who embrace emotional intelligence and vulnerability unlock the potential for dynamic, high-performing teams, fostering collaboration and trust.

Ironically, initiatives designed to promote inclusivity can sometimes leave men feeling excluded or silenced, particularly those in majority groups. The fear of being labelled sexist or racist has led many men to disengage from conversations about diversity and inclusion, perpetuating a cycle of silence and misunderstanding. This paradox reflects society's conflicting messages: men are shaped by patriarchal expectations but are now criticized for embodying them in the workplace.

To break this cycle, organizations must co-design strategies that empower all employees—supporting minority groups while also helping men embrace positive masculine traits like empathy, collaboration, and emotional intelligence. This approach bridges the gap between inclusivity and psychological well-being, enabling men to evolve beyond restrictive norms while contributing meaningfully to diverse cultures.

Fostering a workplace where everyone feels valued and respected, regardless of gender or background, is not just about promoting inclusivity. It is about creating a culture of shared humanity and collective growth. When companies prioritize this deeper level of well-being, they unlock individual potential, organizational resilience, creativity, and success.

5. **Driving Organizational Change:** In the realm of organizational change, CEOs can lead by example in driving initiatives that foster high levels of pro-social behavior—actions intended to benefit others and the broader organization. However, this responsibility extends beyond the CEO to include leaders at all levels. Leaders must embody values such as empathy, inclusivity, and transparency to cultivate a culture conducive to pro-social behavior. By demonstrating these values through their actions and decisions, leaders set the tone for the entire organization.

Leaders who co-design with employees to shape the desired change and facilitate buy-in at all levels. This collaborative approach encourages employee input and feedback, empowering them to drive organizational change actively. Through open dialogue and transparent communication, leaders can build trust and alignment, ensuring the change process is inclusive and supporting employees' psychological well-being.

By embracing a leadership style grounded in empathy and collaboration, CEOs and leaders can create an environment where pro-social behavior thrives, leading to improved organizational performance and employee satisfaction. This shift from hierarchical decision-making to a more inclusive and participatory approach actively drives successful organizational change, while fostering a culture of trust and belonging within the organization.

Navigating the Path to Empowering Organizational Culture

Now, while in theory, we should all desire to have organizational cultures that promote pro-social behavior and high levels of psychological well-being, the reality is that as leaders, we must navigate a minefield of challenges as we humanize to foster a workplace culture that allows all individuals to thrive. This requires resilience and an understanding of how masculine psychology, with its focus on strength, protection, and problem-solving, plays a critical role in this process. Leaders must channel these attributes to confront challenges head-on, protect the well-being of their teams, and build structures that enable collective success. By combining the resilience rooted in masculine psychology with the empathy and community-building strengths of feminine psychology, we can foster a balanced approach to leadership that empowers individuals and organizations to flourish.

As we delve into the challenges leaders encounter in driving inclusive cultures, it's crucial to highlight the foundational principle that profit or KPIs are not merely a goal in itself but rather an outcome of organizational culture. Culture is the bedrock upon which engaged and motivated employees stand, poised to deliver tangible results. At its core, culture embodies the values of respect, recognition, and a sense of belonging—factors that inspire individuals to contribute their best and align their efforts with the organization's mission. So, as we work to overcome the challenges ahead, it is important to come back to the 'why' workplace culture is critical to the organization's prosperity.

The ultimate aim is to cultivate a compelling culture so employees feel valued and appreciated to the point where they envision a future where they would encourage their loved ones to work at the organization, thereby generating generational employment. It's about creating an environment that attracts talent magnetically, driving revenue and profit through a workforce deeply committed to the organization's success. Conversely, neglecting culture can lead to significant financial and cultural costs, resulting from disengagement, staff turnover, and missed opportunities eroding at our bottom lines.

The challenges we encounter as leaders in transforming organizational culture are intricately tied to the human condition. This irony arises from our pursuit of creating environments where individuals can thrive, yet our inherent human tendencies often obstruct the very progress we seek. Resistance to change is a natural human response, rooted in familiarity and apprehension of the unknown. Our negativity bias further complicates this, as people are predisposed to focus on potential losses or risks rather than the benefits of change, amplifying fears and skepticism. Likewise, unconscious biases—such as confirmation bias or in-group bias—can impede efforts to create an inclusive environment, perpetuating patterns of exclusion and inequality. Recognizing and addressing these biases is critical for leaders to foster trust, overcome resistance, and create a culture where all individuals feel valued and empowered to adapt and grow.

In larger organizations, the challenge of scalability looms large. What works seamlessly for a small team may prove unwieldy or ineffective when applied to a multinational corporation with diverse geographies and cultural contexts. Building an empowering organizational culture is not a one-size-fits-all, one-and-done process but a dynamic and continuous journey. As teams evolve, organizations grow or contract, societal contexts shift, and the culture must adapt to remain relevant and effective.

For instance, integrating a Gen Z employee into a team primarily composed of Gen X or Millennials often requires adjustments to accommodate different communication styles, values, and expectations. Similarly, adding a woman to an all-male team may necessitate shifts to ensure inclusivity and psychological safety. These examples highlight that organizational culture must remain flexible, responsive, and intentionally managed to account for such changes.

Therefore, adaptability and continuous evolution are imperative, requiring leaders to remain agile in their approach, actively listen to their teams, and refine strategies to suit the ever-changing landscape of their workforce and the world around them.

The forthcoming chapters of this book are equipped with the essential tools to aid you in surmounting the challenges you encounter, both personally and organizationally, as you embark on the transformative journey of shaping your culture.

As we close out this chapter, it's critical to highlight that organizational culture is not solely the CEO's responsibility. While CEOs play a pivotal role in setting the tone, vision, and strategic direction, "pinning the tail on the CEO" oversimplifies the complexities of culture management. Culture is every employee's responsibility—leaders and team members alike must actively contribute to fostering an environment where values align, collaboration thrives, and everyone feels empowered.

The CEO's Role and the Collective Responsibility

CEOs are uniquely positioned as cultural architects, influencing the organization's priorities and behaviors. They embody the organization's values, communicate a compelling vision, and lead with integrity. However, the CEO cannot single-handedly build or sustain a thriving culture. At every level, executives, managers, and supervisors, leaders must act as stewards of culture within their teams, modelling the behaviors they wish to see and aligning actions with organizational goals.

Team members, too, play a critical role. Through daily interactions, shared experiences, and mutual support, they co-create the lived experience of organizational culture. This shared responsibility ensures that culture becomes a cohesive, collective effort rather than a top-down directive.

Linking Culture and Profit:
The Compounding Effect

Organizational culture is a driving force behind profitability. Employees are more engaged, productive, and innovative when culture fosters psychological well-being, inclusivity, and a sense of belonging. Research has shown that businesses with strong cultures are more likely to achieve financial success. A study by Gallup found that highly engaged teams show 21% greater profitability, underscoring the link between culture and bottom-line performance.

Moreover, culture has a compounding effect. When employees feel valued and psychologically safe, they are more likely to stay with the organization, reducing costly turnover. They also become brand ambassadors, attracting top talent and contributing to a cycle of sustained success. Conversely, neglecting culture leads to disengagement, high turnover, and lost revenue—issues that cost businesses billions annually.

The Power of Psychological Safety

Psychological safety is a cornerstone of a thriving culture. Organizations unlock their full potential when employees feel safe to express ideas, share feedback, and admit mistakes without fear of retaliation. Innovation flourishes, collaboration deepens, and teams become resilient in the face of challenges. Leaders play a crucial role in cultivating this safety, requiring courage, self-awareness, and a willingness to lead with empathy and vulnerability.

The Courage to Reflect and Act

As leaders, we must have the courage to look in the mirror and examine where we need to grow. Are we fostering environments where people feel safe, respected, and valued? Are we willing to confront our own biases and blind spots? Leadership is not about perfection but the willingness to evolve and take action.

Prioritizing culture requires leaders to embrace continuous improvement, listen to diverse perspectives, and take deliberate steps toward inclusivity and psychological well-being. By doing so, we address the *Billion Dollar Blind Spot* and create organizations where people want to work, contribute, and thrive.

A Collaborative Journey

In fostering organizational culture, we must move from the mindset of individual responsibility to collective empowerment. By co-designing culture with employees at every level, we ensure that it reflects the values, needs, and aspirations of the entire workforce. This collaborative approach strengthens buy-in, commitment, and alignment, paving the way for sustainable success.

So, let us embark on this transformative journey together, recognizing that building a thriving organizational culture is not a destination but an ongoing process. By embracing our shared responsibility, linking culture to profit, and prioritizing psychological safety, we can create workplaces where everyone thrives—one courageous step at a time.

The Path We Have Walked

The farther backward you can look,
the farther forward you are likely to see
—Winston Churchill

To envision a future of equality and inclusivity, we must first understand the lessons of our past. The threads of history weave together to shape our present and future, providing a foundation from which to build a more equitable world. As an Australian woman, I am proud of my homeland's role in the global fight for human equality. In 1902, Australia became the first nation to grant women the dual rights to vote and stand for parliament—a groundbreaking achievement that set a precedent for progress worldwide. Churchill's words remind us that looking back is not merely an act of reflection but a catalyst for forward momentum.

This historical pride became deeply personal when I discovered a remarkable chapter in my own family's story.

In 1890 and 1891, Sir Henry Parkes, my great-great-great-grandfather, championed electoral reform bills in the New South Wales Parliament that included provisions granting women the right to vote. Known as the "Father of Federation," Parkes played a pivotal role in uniting Australia's colonies and shaping its identity. Alongside his efforts for federation, he was also a vocal advocate for women's rights over 130 years ago.

This revelation stirred a profound sense of responsibility in me. It was a reminder that champions from unexpected quarters have long carried forward the fight for equality. Men like Sir Henry Parkes stood as allies in the fight for women's rights, challenging norms and demonstrating that progress is a collective effort requiring solidarity from all genders. Their actions underscore a timeless truth: true progress transcends gender and demands unified action.

Lessons from Across the Globe

The efforts of pioneers worldwide mirror Australia's journey toward equality. In the United States, Frederick Douglass, an abolitionist and statesman, extended his advocacy beyond racial justice to include women's suffrage. Recognizing the intrinsic link between racial and gender equality, Douglass famously declared, "Right is of no sex—truth is of no color." His impassioned speeches galvanized support for women's rights, reinforcing the necessity of unity in pursuing justice.

Similarly, Susan B. Anthony and Elizabeth Cady Stanton laid the groundwork for women's suffrage in America. Their tireless campaigning and organization paved the way for the 19th Amendment, granting women the right to vote. Male and female figures demonstrate that allyship and advocacy are not confined to a single group but are shared responsibilities that drive meaningful change.

A Collective Humanize

As we reflect on these historical figures, it becomes clear that allyship remains essential. Celebrating male allies is not about diminishing the contributions of women but about recognizing that the journey toward equality is one we must take together. This principle extends beyond the suffrage movement into the modern workplace, where allyship can transform organizational culture.

Today, as we grapple with complex challenges in corporate leadership, the lessons of the past remind us of the power of unity. The fight for gender equality has evolved, encompassing broader concepts like inclusivity, psychological safety, and mutual respect. These values are foundational to thriving organizational cultures that harness their teams' diverse strengths and perspectives.

Translating History to Modern Leadership

In corporate leadership, we often overlook the parallels between historical advocacy and the modern push for inclusive workplace cultures. Just as historical figures leveraged their positions to amplify marginalized voices, today's leaders must use their influence to break down systemic barriers and foster environments where everyone can thrive.

Allyship in the workplace means more than supporting women; it involves building bridges across all forms of diversity. It requires recognizing that equality is not a zero-sum game but a shared endeavor where the success of one contributes to the success of all. This perspective is vital in male-dominated industries, where breaking down traditional norms can pave the way for greater innovation, collaboration, and resilience.

Culture Is Everyone's Responsibility

The responsibility for shaping organizational culture cannot rest solely on the shoulders of the CEO. While CEOs play a pivotal role in setting the tone and direction, the true power of culture lies in collective action. Culture is not static; it evolves with the organization's people, growth, and societal context. Teams within organizations often have unique subcultures that reflect their functions—for example, the ambitious, risk-taking ethos of a sales team compared to the conservative, detail-oriented approach of a finance team. These subcultures must align with the overarching organizational culture to create a cohesive whole.

This alignment requires active participation from leaders at every level. Managers, team leads, and individual contributors all play roles in fostering a culture of respect, collaboration, and psychological safety. When everyone takes ownership of the culture, it becomes a living, breathing entity that adapts to challenges and opportunities.

The Compounding Effect of Culture

Organizational culture has a compounding effect on both human and financial capital. Companies prioritizing psychological safety and employee well-being see measurable benefits, from higher engagement and retention rates to increased innovation and profitability. Research from Gallup highlights that organizations with high employee engagement are 21% more profitable than their less-engaged counterparts.

Psychological safety, a key component of culture, empowers employees to speak up, share ideas, and take calculated risks without fear of retribution. This openness fosters pro-social behavior, where individuals actively support one another and align their efforts with organizational goals. The result is a workplace where people feel valued and motivated to contribute their best.

Courage and Reflection

Creating such cultures requires courage from leaders to reflect on their own practices and growth areas. It demands a willingness to confront unconscious biases and challenge traditional norms. Leaders must ask themselves tough questions: Are my actions fostering inclusivity? Am I creating an environment where all voices are heard? Do I empower my team to bring their authentic selves to work?

As leaders, we must have the courage to look in the mirror and take action where necessary. This self-awareness is the cornerstone of authentic leadership, which inspires trust and drives sustainable change. By embodying empathy, vulnerability, and a commitment to inclusivity, leaders can build cultures that not only address the billion-dollar issue of poor workplace culture but also unlock the full potential of their organizations.

Moving Forward

The path we have walked teaches us that working together makes progress possible. As we honor the legacy of pioneers like Sir Henry Parkes and Frederick Douglass, let us also embrace the responsibility we carry as leaders. By fostering cultures of respect, inclusivity, and psychological safety, we can create workplaces that reflect the best of humanity—environments where everyone, regardless of gender or background, can thrive.

Together, let us move forward with determination and optimism, knowing that our collective efforts have the power to shape a brighter, more equitable future for all.

PART 2

The Respect Equality Model (REM)

Navigating Adversity with PERMA

Well-being cannot exist in your own head.
Well-being is a combination of feeling good
as well as actually having meaning,
good relationships and accomplishments
—Martin Seligman

In life and leadership, moments of adversity repeatedly test the limits of our resilience and resolve. For me, one such moment came when I was lying in my hospital bed after the accident, uncertain if I would ever walk again. The weight of that uncertainty was crushing; it's what forced me to reassess myself and what it took to be strong and successful in the face of life-altering challenges. It was in this crucible of adversity that I discovered a lifeline: positive psychology and the PERMA framework.

The traditional focus in psychology, as with diversity, has been on identifying and addressing problems. It's a mindset that involves identifying a problem so you can fix it. The trouble is that in psychology, as in workplace diversity efforts, this often has the effect of focusing excessively on what's wrong rather than what's right. Positive psychology takes a different approach. Its goal is to promote well-being and improving everyday life. Psychologist Martin Seligman launched the modern positive psychology movement in 1999, a movement which has become internationally prominent and has led to the development of a framework which outlines five pillars of well-being: Positive Emotions, Engagement, Relationships, Meaning, and Accomplishment (PERMA).

PERMA was more than a concept I read about—it became my survival guide in business and life. In my darkest moments, these pillars weren't abstract ideas but actionable steps that lit my path forward.

This framework shaped my recovery and transformed my approach to leadership. Day by day, hour by hour, I wove these principles into my life and work, discovering that even the smallest actions rooted in these pillars could spark monumental change. Whether facing personal adversity or navigating workplace challenges, PERMA has proven to be a roadmap for resilience, growth, and transformational success.

For leaders today, the *Billion Dollar Blind Spot* demands more than survival—it calls for thriving. By integrating PERMA into how we lead, we can foster environments where our people feel empowered, connected, and capable of achieving extraordinary results.

Let's dive into the five pillars of PERMA, exploring how they can revolutionize how we lead and empower our teams to thrive, addressing challenges with courage and purpose.

The Five Pillars of PERMA:
A Personal Lens Positive Emotions

Positive emotions aren't about addressing hardship with fake positivity; they're about finding light even in the shadows. When I was in recovery, moments of joy came within my darkness from the simplest things—a kind word from a nurse, the warmth of sunlight streaming through a window. In leadership, I channel this by starting meetings with gratitude, acknowledging the efforts of my team, and celebrating small wins. For instance, I've found that recognizing a colleague's creative solution to a problem can lift morale and inspire others to contribute more freely.

In practice, cultivating positive emotions in the workplace means intentionally creating spaces for optimism. This could be as simple as incorporating gratitude exercises during team check-ins or celebrating milestones, no matter how small. These moments build an emotional foundation that helps teams weather challenges with resilience.

Positive Emotions:
Lighting the Path in Uncertainty

When I was learning to walk again, there were days when the weight of despair threatened to overshadow every flicker of hope. Yet, amidst those moments, there were glimmers of joy—a nurse who cheered me on when I took two unsteady steps or the golden sunlight through a window that reminded me the world was still turning. Positive emotions didn't erase my struggles; they gave me the strength to face them.

In the workplace, this same principle holds. Leaders have the unique opportunity to create those moments of joy and gratitude for their teams. Imagine starting a team meeting by sharing a small win or expressing gratitude for someone's effort. Recently, I saw a team member light up when I acknowledged the creative solution they contributed to a complex problem. It wasn't a grand gesture, but it sparked energy and engagement that rippled through the team.

Beyond simple acknowledgments, fostering positivity can be transformative. One organization implemented a gratitude board where employees could publicly thank their colleagues. What started as a quiet corner in the office became a buzzing hub of appreciation, shifting the team's dynamic from competitive to collaborative.

Your Action: Bring light into your workplace. Start meetings with gratitude. Celebrate even the smallest successes. Show that even amidst challenges, there is room for joy.

Engagement

Engagement is about being so immersed in what you're doing that time seems to stand still. I remember the hours I spent relearning to walk, fully present in each small movement. Those moments demanded my total focus, leaving no room for fear or doubt. As a leader, I strive to help my team find that same sense of flow in their work. This means aligning tasks with individual strengths and passions.

To foster engagement, I ensure my team members are challenged in ways that stretch their abilities without overwhelming them. For example, I worked with one team member to reimagine their role by incorporating creative projects they were passionate about. Not only did their engagement soar, but their innovative ideas became a catalyst for organizational success.

Engagement:
The Power of Flow

Do you remember the last time you were so absorbed in what you were doing that you lost track of time? For me, this happened during hours of painstaking rehab. Each movement, no matter how small, required my full focus. There was no space for fear or doubt—just the task at hand. That state of flow became my refuge and my triumph.

In leadership, engagement is about creating that same immersive experience for your team. It's about aligning their tasks with their strengths and passions. I once worked with a colleague who was struggling with a role that didn't excite them. By reworking their responsibilities to include more creative projects, their enthusiasm soared. Their newfound engagement sparked ideas that reshaped the way we approached marketing campaigns.

But engagement isn't just about matching skills to tasks—it's about challenging your team to grow. Stretch assignments that push someone out of their comfort zone, while still offering support, can transform disengagement into inspiration. Think of it as guiding them into a flow state where work feels meaningful, not mechanical.

Your Action: Ask your team: "What challenges excite you?" and "How can we make your work more fulfilling?"

Then, craft roles and opportunities that align with their answers.

Relationships

If engagement is the fire that fuels us, relationships are the hearth that keeps us grounded. During my recovery, the unwavering support of my family, friends, and medical team gave me the courage to keep going. In leadership, relationships are the foundation for trust and collaboration. I make it a priority to create psychological safety, where team members feel heard and valued.

A practical example of fostering relationships is through regular one-on-one check-ins. These aren't just about performance; they're opportunities to understand personal goals and challenges. When one employee struggled to balance work and family life, we worked together to find a solution that supported their personal and professional needs. That level of care fosters loyalty and a deeper commitment to the team's shared vision.

Relationships:
The Heartbeat of Leadership

During my recovery, relationships were my anchor. Family, friends, and even my physical therapists became the scaffolding that held me up when I felt like crumbling. The same holds true in the workplace—relationships are the foundation of trust, collaboration, and resilience.

I've learned that one-on-one check-ins aren't just a nice-to-have but essential. During one such meeting, a team member confided their struggle to balance work and family. We worked out a flexible schedule that allowed them to thrive at both. That moment of care didn't just solve a problem—it deepened trust and commitment.

Building relationships also means fostering connections across the team. At *Empowered Women in Trades*, we moved beyond traditional team-building exercises. Instead, we hosted a family-inclusive BBQ. Watching colleagues' kids play together while their parents shared stories reminded me of how connection strengthens individuals and the whole organization.

Your Action: Build genuine relationships. Schedule regular one-on-ones focused on understanding—not just managing—your team. Encourage shared experiences that build trust and connection.

Meaning

Finding meaning is about connecting our actions to a greater purpose. For me, every painful step in recovery was a testament to the possibility of transformation. As a leader, I work to infuse meaning into our work by aligning individual goals with the organization's mission. For example, at Empowered Women in Trades, our mission to break down gender barriers gives every task—no matter how routine—a sense of purpose.

Leaders can create meaning by helping team members see how their contributions impact the bigger picture. In one instance, I connected a marketing coordinator's campaign success to the larger goal of increasing gender representation in trades. Their pride in that connection spurred them to take on even greater challenges with enthusiasm.

Meaning:
The Why Behind the Work

What gets you out of bed in the morning? For me, it's the knowledge that I'm helping to break down barriers for women in trades. That purpose turns even the toughest days into meaningful steps forward. Purpose isn't just about the big picture; it's about finding significance in every action.

At *Empowered Women in Trades*, every recruitment campaign we run ties back to our mission of gender equity. I remember explaining to a marketing coordinator how their successful ad campaign directly contributed to a rise in applications from women apprentices. Watching their pride and excitement was a powerful reminder of how connecting tasks to a greater purpose energizes people.

This isn't just a nice idea—it's a necessity. When people see their work as meaningful, they're more resilient, creative, and committed. It's about showing them that what they do matters, not just to the organization but to the world.

Your Action: Share stories that tie daily tasks to the organization's mission. Regularly remind your team why their work matters.

Accomplishment

Accomplishment isn't just about grand victories; it's about recognizing progress, however small. I'll never forget the day I took my first unassisted step after months of effort. That moment wasn't just a milestone; it was fuel for every step that followed. In leadership, I use accomplishment to build momentum. Celebrating team wins—whether it's landing a new client or mastering a new tool—reinforces confidence and resilience.

To instill this in your workplace, set clear, achievable goals and celebrate when they're met. One way I've done this is by creating a "Wall of Wins" where team members can share their achievements, big or small. This simple practice not only recognizes individual effort but also fosters a collective sense of pride and motivation.

Accomplishment:
Fueling Forward Momentum

I'll never forget the moment I took my first unassisted step. That single step wasn't just a milestone; it was proof of progress and a promise of what was to come. In leadership, recognizing accomplishments—big or small—fuels this same momentum.

At one point, we created a "Wall of Wins" at *Empowered Women in Trades*. Team members added sticky notes for every achievement, from securing a new partner to finishing a challenging report. Watching the wall fill up was more than motivational—it was a tangible reminder of our collective progress.

Recognition doesn't always have to be public. A handwritten note or a private acknowledgment can carry immense weight. When I personally thanked an apprentice for mentoring a younger colleague, their surprised smile said it all. That simple act reinforced their sense of accomplishment and inspired them to keep leading.

Your Action: Celebrate progress. Whether it's a wall of wins, a team email, or a simple thank-you note, show your team that every step forward counts.

Embracing PERMA:
A Roadmap for Thriving Leadership

PERMA is more than a framework for personal resilience; it's a transformative leadership philosophy. By embedding pillars into your daily practices, you can create workplaces that are inclusive, empowering, thriving and profitable.

Great change starts with small actions. As you reflect on these pillars, ask yourself:

How can I infuse joy into my team's day?

How can I align their strengths with meaningful work?

How can I nurture connections and celebrate progress?

The answers to these questions hold the power to dismantle the *Billion Dollar Blind Spot* and unlock the untapped potential within your organization.

Through the lens of the PERMA framework, I learned to embrace the full spectrum of human experience the pain and the joy, the challenges and the triumphs. It became the backbone of my entrepreneurial journey, guiding me as I navigated the complexities of building a business while confronting ongoing health challenges. What began as a personal lifeline in my darkest moments has evolved into a powerful roadmap for leadership and organizational well-being.

As leaders, we must also navigate our fears and uncertainties—whether about driving inclusivity, challenging the status quo, or addressing systemic issues like gender diversity. The PERMA framework offers more than just a theoretical guide; it's a practical toolkit for transforming discomfort into growth. It begins with acknowledging emotions—whether apprehension, doubt, or fear of inadequacy—and leaning into them with curiosity and compassion. This openness is essential for fostering innovation and making meaningful progress. And for that to work, you need an environment where people feel safe expressing those emotions.

Let's look next at why it's important to foster a workplace environment where openness is not only allowed, but encouraged and supported.

Psychological Safety

As I mentioned earlier, my approach in my professional life and personal riding competition was to adopt a "masculine" set of behaviors and mindsets. Recovering from my accident forced me to reevaluate a lot of things, which led to my embracing of an integrated, holistic approach to the unique strengths of men and women. Would I have done so had I not been forced to hit a big "reset" button on my life? It's hard to say. But there's a reason that so many people unthinkingly adopt the idea that it's necessary to suppress emotions and reactions in the workplace: a lack of psychological safety.

Psychological safety is a space where individuals feel safe to express vulnerability and explore deeper emotions without fear of judgment. It's not a framework or action item per se—it's an outcome of the PERMA model, a necessary corollary to the idea of focusing on the positive rather than the negative. Have you ever been in a meeting where a colleague was presenting something with which you disagreed, but you kept quiet? Maybe you did so because that colleague is a supervisor; maybe it's because you didn't want to seem like you weren't a team player. Maybe you didn't want others to criticize you—often workplaces reward those who tear down coworkers in this way. Maybe (if you're a man) you didn't want to seem weak by expressing concerns; maybe (if you're a woman) you didn't want others to think you weren't as strong as they. If any of this rings a bell, then you've experienced a workplace culture which lacks psychological safety.

This is actually a critical part of any workplace culture reform, because you cannot address the issues of interpersonal dynamics if people don't feel free to do so. Put another way, psychological safety means that people feel free to provide feedback, to collaborate effectively.

The Role of Feedback Loops and Psychological Safety:
A Positive Psychology Lens

Feedback is more than a mechanism for improvement—it is a tool for empowerment. In male-dominated industries, where women and marginalized groups often face additional challenges, the creation of robust feedback loops grounded in psychological safety can serve as a catalyst for genuine inclusion and growth. As defined by

Dr. Amy Edmondson, psychological safety is the belief that one can speak up, offer ideas, or admit mistakes without fear of humiliation or punishment. This principle aligns seamlessly with the tenets of positive psychology, emphasizing strengths, growth, and resilience over fear and avoidance.

The Power of Positive Psychology in Feedback Loops

Positive psychology reframes feedback from a critique of past actions to a forward-focused opportunity for growth and fulfilment. In this context, feedback becomes not about highlighting weaknesses but about recognizing strengths, addressing gaps constructively, and fostering a shared commitment to continuous improvement.

When employees feel that feedback highlights their potential and equips them with actionable strategies, they are more likely to embrace it, even in challenging circumstances. This is particularly transformative for underrepresented groups, as it shifts the narrative from mere tolerance to genuine empowerment and inclusion.

Think back to the Ladder of Inference. The space between the rungs of that decision-making process are where psychological safety, or its lack, comes into play. If other people aren't free to add perspective or opinion, or if the decision maker doesn't feel free admitting any limitations, hesitation, or uncertainty, that's a sign of insufficient psychological safety. Conversely, in an environment where people are more open, it's easier to recognize and overcome our innate biases.

A focus on PERMA will automatically improve psychological safety. It prioritizes acceptance and focusing on the positive, rather than punishing or reacting negatively to input that doesn't align with expectations.

This isn't something vague and aspirational. Psychologically safe workplace cultures are measurably more productive and innovative and have reduced turnover. To put it in terms of the bottom line, teams that value psychological safety outperform those that don't; leaders who embrace their humanity inspire loyalty, creativity, and resilience. It's that simple.

Navigating Fear:
Cultivating Psychological Safety for Gender respect in Traditional Workplaces.

Leaders initiating cultural transformation in workplaces embedded in traditional masculine norms often face a spectrum of perceived fears. These can include apprehensions about disrupting deeply entrenched norms and encountering resistance and personal insecurities about their ability to effect meaningful change. Such fears are rooted in the fear of social rejection, which is a primal human instinct linked to our evolutionary need for belonging. Overcoming these fears requires self-awareness and deliberate actions to foster an environment where trust and collaboration can flourish.

Pro-social behavior, defined as voluntary actions that benefit others, is pivotal in creating this environment. These behaviors—ranging from offering help to expressing empathy—are instrumental in establishing psychological safety. Psychological safety is the foundation for a culture where individuals feel empowered to express ideas, take risks, and show vulnerability without fear of negative consequences such as ridicule or rejection. This sense of safety is especially crucial for advancing gender respect, as it encourages open dialogue and challenges the biases that often underpin traditional workplace norms.

Cultivating psychological safety goes beyond surface-level gestures; leaders must model vulnerability and authenticity, demonstrating a commitment to inclusivity and mutual respect. For example, a leader might openly acknowledge their own learning curve in understanding gender dynamics, which humanizes them and encourages team members to share their perspectives and challenges. Such openness creates a ripple effect, fostering a culture where diverse voices feel valued and heard.

Ultimately, leaders can dismantle barriers to inclusion by addressing the root causes of fear—whether tied to social rejection or resistance to change—and actively promoting pro-social behavior. This approach enables every team member to contribute fully and authentically, transforming workplace culture into one that thrives on collaboration, innovation, and respect for all individuals, regardless of gender or background.

Our interpretation of situations significantly shapes our emotional responses, underscoring the importance of creating workplace cultures prioritizing psychological safety and fostering high-quality connections. These connections, pivotal in promoting pro-social behavior—actions aimed at benefiting others—lay the groundwork for a supportive environment where team members feel valued, understood, and empowered. Cultivating such a culture encourages openness, reduces fear, and enables individuals to engage fully, contributing to a more inclusive and equitable workplace. This approach enhances individual well-being and drives organizational success by leveraging diverse perspectives and talents.

To create trust and psychological safety in teams, it's vital to understand and apply the research findings of scholars like Amy Edmondson, who emphasizes the significance of fostering an environment where team members feel safe to express their ideas, take risks, and admit mistakes without fear of repercussions. Strategies for nurturing positive relationships include encouraging open communication, demonstrating empathy, actively seeking diverse perspectives, and showing appreciation for team contributions. These actions help build a foundation of trust, which is crucial for psychological safety and enabling teams to thrive in a supportive and inclusive culture.

The 4 Stages of Psychological Safety

Timothy Clark's framework on psychological safety, outlined in *"The 4 Stages of Psychological Safety: Defining the Path to Inclusion and Innovation,"* offers a clear roadmap for creating inclusive and innovative workplaces. The framework identifies four stages: **Inclusion Safety**, where individuals feel safe to be themselves; **Learner Safety**, which encourages learning and growth; **Contributor Safety**, empowering individuals to add value; and **Challenger Safety**, enabling team members to question the status quo without fear. Each stage is critical for fostering a culture of openness, respect, and continuous improvement. Here's how each stage can be applied, with practical examples to bring them to life:

Inclusion Safety:
Creating Spaces for Belonging

Inclusion Safety ensures individuals feel welcomed and valued for who they are. This is especially important in male-dominated industries, where underrepresented groups may feel marginalized. For instance, a company could establish **mentorship programs** that pair women with industry veterans, breaking down barriers and fostering a sense of belonging. Another example is organizing **team-building activities** celebrating diverse contributions, such as cultural appreciation days or collaborative workshops highlighting unique team strengths. Encouraging **open discussions about gender dynamics** in facilitated sessions can further challenge stereotypes, helping shift organizational culture toward inclusivity.

Learner Safety:
Supporting Growth Without Judgment

Learner Safety creates an environment where individuals feel safe to experiment, ask questions, and learn from mistakes. This can particularly encourage women to take on roles or projects outside their traditional comfort zones. For example, **mentorship and sponsorship programs** can offer women the chance to acquire new technical skills or leadership experience in a supportive setting. Implementing **constructive feedback systems**, where mistakes are reframed as learning opportunities rather than failures, fosters a growth mindset. A practical initiative could include **failure-sharing sessions**, where team members discuss what went wrong, what they learned, and how to improve, building confidence and resilience.

Contributor Safety:
Empowering Meaningful Contributions

Contributor Safety allows individuals to bring their best ideas and efforts to the table without fear of being overshadowed or dismissed. This can be achieved by granting **autonomy in decision-making** while providing adequate guidance. For example, creating **cross-functional project teams** and appointing women as project leads allows them to contribute outside their traditional roles, showcasing their skills. Implementing **recognition programs** that celebrate both large achievements and incremental successes ensures that all contributions are valued. For instance, a "Strengths Spotlight" segment in meetings can highlight how team members' unique strengths positively impacted a project.

Challenger Safety:
Encouraging Constructive Dissent

Challenger Safety empowers individuals to question established norms and propose innovative ideas without fear of retribution. This is particularly critical for advancing gender respect, as it allows employees to address unconscious biases and suggest improvements. For instance, a company could host **open forums or anonymous suggestion boxes** to gather input on workplace policies or practices that may unintentionally favor one gender. By encouraging and protecting such candid discussions, leaders can shape inclusivity initiatives based on the insights of all employees, ensuring changes are meaningful and widely supported. A specific example might include a review of hiring practices, where employees collaboratively identify ways to make recruitment processes more equitable.

The Results of Psychological Safety

The workplace transforms into a dynamic, inclusive environment when these stages are fully implemented. Employees feel seen, valued, and empowered to innovate. Fear diminishes, trust strengthens, and the organization becomes better equipped to tackle challenges, foster collaboration, and drive meaningful cultural change. Psychological safety becomes not just a goal but a powerful catalyst for sustained success and respect for all.

Central to this transformation is the interplay between fear and psychological safety. Leaders must navigate their own and their team's instinctual responses to change, recognizing the primal roots of fear and implementing strategies to foster a culture of openness and resilience. Cultivating high-quality connections and encouraging pro-social behavior further enhance psychological safety, creating an environment where all individuals feel valued, heard, and empowered to contribute their best.

Understanding the stages of psychological safety outlined by Timothy Clark provides a roadmap for creating inclusive and innovative workplaces. From inclusion safety to challenger safety, each stage represents a progression towards a culture where everyone feels welcomed, valued, and encouraged to share their ideas and perspectives. Initiatives such as mentorship programs, feedback systems focused on growth, and open forums for constructive disagreement play crucial roles in advancing gender respect and fostering a culture of continuous improvement.

Ultimately, the journey towards gender respect requires leaders to challenge entrenched cultural norms, navigate fears of rejection and personal inadequacy, and cultivate an environment where every voice is valued and respected. By embracing empathy, fostering psychological safety, and nurturing high-quality connections, organizations can unleash the transformative potential inherent in diverse and inclusive workplaces, driving towards a future where gender respect flourishes and organizational success is synonymous with inclusivity and equity.

The Art of Appreciative Inquiry

*Change is the law of life. And those who look only to
the past or present are certain to miss the future*
—John F. Kennedy

The PERMA framework provides constructive goals for shifting workplace culture in a positive direction. Let me show you how I used a specific approach to help implement it with a client: appreciative inquiry.

In the bustling city of Melbourne, Australia, amidst the towering edifices of corporate power, lies a company's headquarters on the brink of transformation. Here, in the heart of the city's vibrant business district, "David," a seasoned executive, finds himself at a crossroads. As he gazes out of his office window, he can't shake the weight of the question looming over him: How can he navigate his organization through the tumultuous seas of change, particularly with regards to gender diversity?

For David, the challenge runs deeper than mere

corporate strategy or bottom-line metrics. It's a deeply personal journey that stirs emotions he's long kept buried beneath layers of professionalism. As a male leader in a traditionally male-dominated industry, David grapples with conflicting emotions of responsibility and uncertainty. On the one hand, he feels a sense of duty to champion diversity and inclusion within his organization, recognizing the moral imperative of creating a workplace where everyone feels valued and respected, regardless of gender. On the other hand, he's acutely aware of the roadblocks and resistance he may encounter along the way.

Navigating the shifting landscape of gender diversity isn't just a matter of implementing policies or initiatives—it's about confronting entrenched norms and challenging the status quo. David knows that change won't come easily, especially in an environment where long-standing traditions and ingrained biases are deeply entrenched. The fear of colleague resistance, skepticism from stakeholders, and even his own internal doubts weigh heavily on his mind, casting a shadow over his confidence.

David isn't alone in his quest for answers or his experience navigating this challenge. Clients seeking guidance and support often present this question to me, eager to uncover strategies that will empower them to navigate this uncharted territory of improving gender diversity with confidence and clarity.

Together, David and I delve into the depths of organizational theory and change management models, searching for insights that will illuminate the path forward. In this exploration, we encounter an intriguing concept: Appreciative Inquiry (AI), a strengths-based approach to organizational change that focuses on identifying and amplifying what is already working well within an organization. Developed by David Cooperrider and Suresh Srivastava in the 1980s, AI is grounded in the belief that organizations grow and evolve in the direction of the questions they ask. Its core principles include:

- **Constructionist Principle**: Reality is socially constructed through language and dialogue. Organizations can co-create a new reality focused on strengths and possibilities by asking positive, generative questions.
- **Simultaneity Principle**: Inquiry and change are simultaneous. As organizations inquire into their strengths and successes, they begin to envision and enact positive change.
- **Poetic Principle**: Organizations are living stories, continually unfolding and evolving. AI encourages organizations to tell stories of their preferred future, inspiring collective action and transformation.
- **Anticipatory Principle**: Images of the future influence organizational behavior in the present. By envisioning a

positive future, organizations can align their actions and behaviors with their desired outcomes.

- **Positive Principle**: Positive emotions and experiences generate positive actions and outcomes. AI seeks to amplify positive emotions, strengths, and successes within organizations to fuel growth and innovation.

By embracing these principles, organizations can foster a culture of positivity, collaboration, and continuous improvement, leading to a psychologically safer work environment and sustainable change and growth.

Intrigued by the potential of AI to revolutionize his approach to change management, David and I found it to be a forward-thinking approach that challenges the conventional wisdom of problem-solving and resistance management that have long dominated the discourse on change.

Through the lens of Appreciative Inquiry, David and I begin to see the changing landscape of gender diversity as an opportunity to be embraced—a chance to tap into their team's collective talents, perspectives, and experiences. It helps us to envision a future where inclusivity reigns, diversity is celebrated, and innovation thrives in the fertile ground of collaboration and respect.

AI can be applied to effectively manage change within organizations, using its 4-D Cycle to guide us through a process of discovery, envisioning, planning, and implementation. By focusing on strengths, opportunities, and possibilities, rather than dwelling on problems and deficits, AI offers a powerful framework for fostering positive change and creating a future where everyone can thrive.

1. **Discovery**: In this phase, organizations identify and appreciate their existing strengths, successes, and positive experiences. Through open dialogue and inquiry, stakeholders explore what is working well and what gives life to the organization. This discovery process helps build a foundation of positivity and optimism, fostering a shared understanding of the organization's assets and capabilities.

2. **Dream**: Building on the insights gained in the discovery phase, stakeholders envision their desired future. This phase encourages creativity and imagination, inviting participants to dream big and articulate their aspirations for the organization. Stakeholders can generate a compelling vision that inspires and motivates action by focusing on possibilities and desired outcomes, rather than limitations or constraints.

3. **Design**: In the design phase, stakeholders translate their dreams into actionable strategies and plans. This involves collaboratively brainstorming ideas, setting goals, and developing concrete action plans to achieve

the desired future. By leveraging the strengths identified in the discovery phase, organizations can design innovative solutions and interventions that capitalize on their existing assets and resources.

4. **Destiny**: The destiny phase involves implementing and sustaining the changes identified in the design phase. This requires ongoing commitment, effort, and collaboration from all stakeholders to turn the vision into reality. By aligning actions with the organization's values and aspirations, stakeholders can create a future that reflects their shared vision and goals.

Throughout the 4-D Cycle, Appreciative Inquiry focuses on strengths, opportunities, and possibilities rather than problems and deficits—it is in effect an applied form of positive psychology. By adopting a positive and forward-thinking mindset, organizations can unlock their full potential and create a continuous improvement and innovation culture. Instead of dwelling on past failures or shortcomings, AI encourages organizations to embrace their strengths and build upon their successes, driving positive change and development.

Appreciative Inquiry offers a transformative approach to change management, steering organizations away from traditional deficit-based models towards a more positive and empowering paradigm. At its core, it focuses on harnessing individuals' and teams' collective strengths, aspirations, and potential, making it an invaluable tool in navigating complex organizational transitions.

One of the key benefits of using Appreciative Inquiry in change management is its inherent emphasis on positivity and possibility. Unlike traditional change management methodologies that often dwell on problems and deficits, AI starts from a place of strength, focusing on what is working well within the organization and building upon it. By shining a spotlight on successes and achievements, AI cultivates a sense of optimism and confidence among employees, inspiring them to embrace change as an opportunity for growth rather than a threat to stability.

AI uniquely fosters engagement, empowerment, and collaboration during organizational change. By involving stakeholders at all levels—through interviews, focus groups, and participatory workshops—it taps into the collective wisdom and creativity of the workforce. This inclusive approach generates valuable insights, cultivates a sense of ownership, and drives commitment to the change initiative.

AI promotes a culture of collaboration and co-creation, breaking down silos and encouraging cross-functional teamwork. Organizations can craft innovative solutions to complex challenges by uniting diverse perspectives, foster sustainable change, and strengthen relationships. This collaborative process builds resilience and adaptability, critical for navigating today's fast-paced business environment.

Ultimately, AI transcends traditional problem-solving by unlocking the full collaborative potential of individuals and teams. Focusing on strengths, opportunities, and shared aspirations empowers organizations to embrace change as a springboard for growth, innovation, and long-term success.

Applying Appreciative Inquiry in Organizational Culture Change

AI is a helpful framework because it provides a roadmap for implementing PERMA principles in the workplace. Below, we explore how AI can be applied effectively to initiate and sustain cultural change.

1. Initiating Cultural Change

- **Appreciative Inquiry Interviews:** AI interviews can uncover organizational strengths by asking employees across levels and departments about peak performance or successful collaboration moments. For example, a manufacturing company might ask, "Can you describe a time when teamwork led to exceptional results on a project?" This approach reveals key success drivers, such as effective communication or shared goals, which can then be expanded across the organization.

Why: These interviews build an understanding of what works well, fostering a positive mindset from the start.

How: Use open-ended, strengths-focused questions to uncover actionable insights and build trust among participants.

- **Appreciative Workshops:** Hosting workshops or summits with diverse stakeholders can help co-create a shared vision for the future. For instance, in a retail organization aiming to improve customer experience, participants might brainstorm ways to amplify existing practices like personalized service or community engagement.

  Why: Workshops harness collective creativity, ensuring every voice is heard.

  How: Incorporate visioning exercises where participants imagine the organization in five years, emphasizing its ideal state and identifying steps to achieve it.

2. Sustaining Cultural Change

- **Appreciative Interventions:** Implement team-building exercises or peer coaching to embed AI principles into daily interactions. For example, a tech company could organize "gratitude circles" where employees share achievements or acknowledge colleagues' contributions.

Why: Interventions sustain the momentum of cultural change, making positivity a routine practice.

How: Align interventions with existing team practices, like starting meetings with a round of positive reflections or success stories.

- **Strengths-Based Feedback:** A strengths-based feedback system shifts the focus from correcting weaknesses to building on successes. For instance, during performance reviews, a manager might highlight an employee's leadership in cross-departmental collaboration and explore how they can mentor others.

  Why: Recognizing strengths boosts morale and ownership, creating a culture of mutual respect.

  How: Train leaders to provide feedback that aligns with AI principles, celebrating achievements while identifying growth opportunities.

3. Techniques for Conducting AI Interviews, Workshops, and Interventions

- **Framing Questions:** Positive, open-ended questions elicit meaningful responses. For example, in an AI workshop, ask: "What do we do best as a team, and how can we build on that?"

Why: Questions shape the direction of conversations, focusing on possibilities rather than problems.

How: Craft questions around themes like strengths, peak moments, and aspirations to spark creative dialogue.

* **Active Listening:** Fully engaging with participants ensures their insights are heard and valued. For example, a facilitator might paraphrase responses during an AI interview to ensure understanding and encourage deeper sharing.

  Why: Active listening builds trust and ensures participants feel respected.

  How: Use techniques like summarizing and reflective questioning to uncover actionable insights.

* **Co-Creation:** Collaborative brainstorming and ideation ensure diverse input shapes the change process. For instance, in a healthcare organization, co-creation might involve front-line staff designing patient-care initiatives alongside administrators.

  Why: Co-creation fosters a sense of ownership and reduces resistance to change.

  How: Facilitate cross-functional groups to design

strategies, encouraging diverse viewpoints and shared accountability.

Focusing on strengths, engagement, and collaboration builds a workplace culture of positivity, innovation, and continuous growth, ensuring lasting impact and organizational success.

Navigating Resistance and Overcoming Challenges

In the pristine, sunlit expanse of the freshly refurbished boardroom, David took his place at the head of the sleek, mahogany table, flanked by his team of eager change agents. The room hummed with a sense of renewal, mirroring the innovative approach David spearheaded to address the organization's cultural transformation.

The walls, adorned with vibrant artwork depicting themes of growth and collaboration, served as a visual reminder of the fresh perspective they were bringing to the table. The aroma of freshly brewed coffee mingled with the scent of optimism, infusing the atmosphere with palpable energy.

As David glanced around the room, he felt a sense of pride in how far they had come. This wasn't just a meeting but a symbol of their collective commitment to embracing change and fostering a culture of openness, inclusion, and empowerment.

However, David couldn't shake the feeling of responsibility weighing on his shoulders. While he was excited about the potential of the Appreciative Inquiry initiative to revolutionize their organizational culture, he couldn't ignore the potential resistance that often accompanied discussions about change.

His team, though enthusiastic, mirrored his mixed emotions. Some leaned forward eagerly, ready to dive into the details of the rollout plan, while others sat back with furrowed brows, apprehension evident in their body language.

Taking a deep breath, David cleared his throat, ready to address the elephant in the room. He knew that acknowledging the challenges and resistance inherent in any change initiative was the first step toward overcoming them.

But as David began to outline the plan, he noticed the furrowed brows and skeptical glances exchanged among his colleagues. It was clear that not everyone was fully on board with the idea of AI as a catalyst for change.

One team member, let's call him Mark, voiced his concerns first. "I'm not sure about this whole Appreciative Inquiry thing," he admitted, leaning back in his chair with a hint of skepticism. "Isn't it just another management fad? Will it really make a difference?"

David nodded, acknowledging Mark's apprehension. He knew that resistance to change was natural, especially when introducing new methodologies like Appreciative Inquiry. He also knew that overcoming these challenges was essential to the success of their initiative.

Addressing common challenges and resistance encountered when implementing Appreciative Inquiry in change initiatives is crucial for fostering buy-in from stakeholders. Some of the most common challenges include:

1. Skepticism and Resistance: Like Mark, many employees may initially be skeptical about the effectiveness of AI or resistant to change in general. They may question the need for a new approach or doubt its potential impact on the organization.

2. Fear of the Unknown: Change can be intimidating, especially when it involves unfamiliar processes or methodologies. Employees may fear AI disrupting established routines or requiring them to learn new skills, leading to uncertainty and resistance.

3. Lack of Understanding: Misconceptions about AI and its application in organizational change may contribute to resistance. Employees may have limited knowledge or experience with AI, leading to skepticism or reluctance to embrace the approach.

To overcome these challenges and foster buy-in from stakeholders, David and his team implemented several strategies:

1. Education and Communication: David took the time to educate his team about AI, its principles, and its potential benefits for the organization. By providing clear and concise communication about the initiative, he helped dispel misconceptions and build understanding among team members.
2. Involvement and Participation: David encouraged active involvement and participation from his team throughout the planning and implementation process. By soliciting input, feedback, and ideas from stakeholders, he empowered them to take ownership of the initiative and feel invested in its success.
3. Demonstrating Success: David leveraged pilot projects and small-scale initiatives to demonstrate the effectiveness of AI in driving positive change within the organization. He helped build credibility and momentum for the larger initiative by showcasing tangible results and success stories.

By addressing resistance head-on and implementing strategies to overcome challenges, David and his team successfully navigated the complexities of change and drove meaningful transformation through AI. As the meeting ended, David felt a renewed sense of optimism and excitement for the journey ahead.

My journey with David reflected an application of the principles I'd been exploring. PERMA was a transformative model for me, but it is a conceptual framework. What I wanted to do was devise a roadmap specifically for businesses that clarified the best ways to leverage the strengths of everyone in the workplace. Next, we'll take a look at the core of the approach I developed during my transformative journey: **The Respect Equality Model.**

CHAPTER 8

The Respect Equality Model

We are all different, which is great because we are all unique. Without diversity, life would be very boring.
—Catherine Pulsifer

In a world as rich and varied as ours, the tapestry of diversity weaves humanity's essence together. Each thread, every hue, contributes to the vibrant mosaic of life.

As we delve into **The Respect Equality Model**, we understand the importance of celebrating and embracing the beauty of our differences while recognizing the common humanity that binds us all. Here's the thing: diversity is more than a moral imperative; *it is a strategic advantage.* Organizations that fail to harness the power of diverse identities and perspectives miss out on innovation, creativity, and collaboration—key elements that drive competitive advantage in today's global economy.

This model acts as a guiding light, illuminating the path toward inclusivity, understanding, and respect in our organizations and communities. By creating environments where everyone feels valued and empowered, the Respect Equality Model addresses the *Billion Dollar Blind Spots* no one is talking about—employee disengagement, high turnover, and lack of innovation. These issues collectively cost organizations billions annually in lost productivity, recruitment, and missed opportunities for growth.

How does it solve the problem?

1. **Retention and Engagement**: Employees who feel respected and included are more likely to stay with their organizations, reducing turnover costs and fostering a sense of loyalty.
2. **Productivity and Well-being**: Psychological safety, a key outcome of the model, enables employees to bring their full selves to work, leading to higher productivity and overall well-being.
3. **Innovation**: Celebrating differences encourages a diversity of thought, unlocking innovative solutions that can drive organizational success.
4. **Profitability**: Research consistently shows that diverse and inclusive companies outperform their less inclusive counterparts in profitability and market share.

The Respect Equality Model empowers organizations to move beyond performative diversity efforts and toward meaningful, systemic change. By recognizing the inherent humanity in all individuals and celebrating their unique contributions, this model provides a blueprint for addressing deep-rooted cultural issues that hinder organizational success.

Through the intentional implementation of such models, we can transform workplace cultures, unlocking not only the financial potential of organizations but also the human potential within them. The Respect Equality Model is the key to building resilient, innovative, and equitable workplaces that thrive in today's dynamic world. It encapsulates the essence of respect, connection, and inclusivity, serving as a guiding light for organizations and individuals striving to create diverse and equitable spaces. It's based on three circles:

1. **Core (Inner Circle)—"Humanity"**
   The foundational principle of the Respect Equality Model begins with recognizing the inherent humanity in each and every individual. At our core, we are all human beings deserving of dignity, empathy, and respect. This inner circle serves as a reminder that regardless of our differences, we share a common humanity that unites us all. It challenges us to look

beyond superficial distinctions and embrace a mindset of gratitude for what we can learn from others who are different from us. Gratitude fosters openness, curiosity, and connection, replacing fear with appreciation.

2. **Middle Circle—"Unique Identities"**
Surrounding the core of humanity is the acknowledgment of our diverse identities. These identities encompass aspects such as gender, sexual orientation, cultural background, and more. While our shared humanity binds us together, our unique identities enrich our collective experiences and perspectives. This middle circle celebrates the beauty of diversity, reminding us that each person's individuality adds value and depth to the fabric of our shared existence. Instead of fearing difference, we must recognize that our psychological resistance often stems from an evolutionary response to perceive "otherness" as a threat. In today's interconnected world, this fear no longer serves us but instead limits our ability to grow and innovate. Overcoming this fear is a critical step in evolving both individually and collectively. Gratitude for diverse identities allows us to see differences as opportunities for growth, rather than as challenges to overcome.

3. **Outer Circle—"Inclusive Actions"**

   The outermost layer of the Respect Equality Model represents the tangible application of respect and inclusivity in our interactions and practices. It encompasses the actions, behaviors, and policies that foster an inclusive environment where every individual feels valued, heard, and respected. By actively practicing inclusivity, we break down barriers, build bridges, and create a culture of psychological safety. This layer is where gratitude transforms into action, as we show appreciation for the strengths and contributions of others by ensuring they have equitable opportunities to thrive.

Why Fear Holds Us Back and Why We Must Evolve Beyond It

The fear of differences often arises from the psychological principle of **in-group vs. out-group bias**—a hardwired tendency to view those who are different from us as "other," triggering feelings of threat or discomfort. While this bias served an evolutionary purpose in early human societies, fostering group cohesion and survival, it now limits our ability to collaborate, innovate, and connect in a diverse and globalized world.

Remaining bound by these fears perpetuates exclusion

and stifles individual and organizational progress. The Respect Equality Model provides a framework to help us evolve beyond these outdated instincts. By acknowledging our shared humanity, celebrating unique identities, and practicing inclusive actions, we can cultivate environments where everyone feels safe, valued, and empowered.

Through gratitude, we shift from fearing differences to appreciating them as the wellspring of strength, resilience, and innovation. When we welcome diverse perspectives, we enrich our understanding, unlock new solutions, and build organizations that are not only more equitable but also more successful in addressing the billion-dollar workplace challenges that stem from disengagement, inequality, and exclusion. By embracing this evolution, we step into a future where respect equality is not just a principle but a lived reality.

From Inclusion to Innovation:
The Respect Equality Model in Action

From inclusive hiring practices to creating spaces for open dialogue and collaboration, the outer circle of the Respect Equality Model embodies the commitment to translating the principles of respect and equality into meaningful action. This model more than a theoretical framework—it's a call to action for leaders to address the

Billion Dollar Blind Spot of disengagement, inequality, and missed opportunities for innovation.

Several years ago, I worked with a diverse team tasked with redesigning an organizational process to improve both efficiency and employee satisfaction. Among the team members were a young woman from a minority cultural background and an older man steeped in decades of industry experience. Initially, their perspectives clashed: his reliance on traditional methods contrasted sharply with her innovative, forward-thinking ideas.

As tension grew, I realized that their conflict wasn't about competence but a fear of change. The older man's reluctance stemmed from feeling his experience was undervalued, while the younger woman struggled with having her ideas dismissed due to her age and background. Drawing on the Respect Equality Model, I began a dialogue that started with acknowledging their shared humanity.

I asked each team member to share what motivated them personally to contribute to the project. As they opened up, the older man expressed a desire to leave a meaningful legacy, while the younger woman shared her vision of breaking barriers for future generations. This moment of mutual understanding allowed them to appreciate their shared goals and unique strengths.

Their collaboration completed the project and exceeded expectations, saving the organization millions annually and increasing employee satisfaction. This experience underscored that diversity, when coupled with inclusivity, unlocks innovation and drives results.

Proactive Inclusivity in the era of Artificial Intelligence

As companies enthusiastically explore the potential of artificial intelligence in their business models, the stakes for inclusive leadership have never been higher. The technology's ability to automate and optimize processes poses a risk of sidelining human creativity, empathy, and emotional intelligence—qualities essential for fostering psychological safety and engagement. It also learns from existing patterns of decision-making and bias, meaning that it will amplify, not counter, workplace culture problems. If leaders fail to manage organizational culture proactively, they risk exacerbating inequalities and alienating employees, compounding the billion-dollar issue of disengagement and inefficiency.

The Respect Equality Model offers a roadmap to address these challenges. Organizations can thrive in this transformative era by recognizing the shared humanity at our core, celebrating unique identities, and committing to inclusive actions.

Three Guiding Questions for Leaders

To ensure respect and equality remain central to their teams, leaders should regularly reflect on the following questions:

1. **How am I acknowledging the humanity of each team member today?**

   Demonstrate empathy and understanding by connecting with team members on a human level, beyond their roles or identities. Small gestures of recognition and care can build trust and loyalty.

2. **In what ways am I celebrating each team member's unique identities and contributions?**

   Embrace the diversity of perspectives and talents within your team. Create opportunities for individuals to showcase their strengths and share their stories, fostering an environment where everyone feels valued.

3. **What actions can I take today to promote inclusivity and belonging within my team?**

   Take tangible steps to foster inclusivity, such as implementing equitable policies, facilitating open dialogue, and championing diversity initiatives. Ensure every team member feels heard and respected.

As leaders, we must move beyond fearing differences and instead show gratitude for the lessons and perspectives they bring. Psychological research shows that fear of difference often stems from uncertainty or a lack of exposure. But by embracing curiosity and understanding, we can evolve past these instincts and create workplaces that thrive on diversity.

In an era of rapid technological and cultural change, the Respect Equality Model is not just a guide but a necessity. It equips organizations to navigate the complexities of modern leadership, ensuring that everyone, regardless of background or identity, has the opportunity to contribute meaningfully. By embracing this model, we can transform the billion-dollar issue of disengagement into an unprecedented opportunity for growth and innovation. Let's create a future where respect and equality are not aspirations but the foundation of thriving organizations.

Championing Human Respect:
The Core of Respect Equality

At the heart of the Respect Equality Model lies a profound belief in the principle of *human respect*—recognizing that every individual possesses inherent dignity, worth, and the capacity to contribute meaningfully to society. Respect Equality extends beyond traditional notions of gender parity, advocating for a world where opportunities, resources, and rights are accessible to all, regardless of their birth or origin.

This philosophy challenges the status quo by fostering an environment where individuals are empowered to assert their agency, make informed choices, and pursue their aspirations without being confined by traditional gender roles or expectations. It is not merely about recognizing individual differences; it is about actively creating spaces where those differences are celebrated as strengths and valued as unique contributions to the collective success of organizations and communities.

In the context of organizational culture, the Respect Equality Model invites leaders to reflect deeply on their practices and actions. When human respect is prioritized, it paves the way for a culture of *mutual empowerment*. In such a culture:

- Empowered men, women, and non-binary individuals uplift each other.
- Harassment, discrimination, and violence are actively addressed and dismantled.
- A foundation of psychological safety allows individuals to express their identity and ideas freely.

By cultivating an environment rooted in respect and understanding, organizations can unlock the full potential of their workforce, driving collaboration, innovation, and sustainable growth.

Why Human Respect Matters More Than Ever

Without intentional action, the same biases that have perpetuated inequality in the past risk becoming embedded in our technological systems. The billion-dollar issue of disengagement, exclusion, and inefficiency in workplaces will only worsen if we fail to prioritize Respect Equality as a foundational value.

Human respect is not just a moral or ethical stance but a proven driver of performance and profitability. Teams that feel valued, included, and respected are more likely to collaborate effectively, innovate boldly, and remain committed to their organization. By addressing barriers to equality and creating safe spaces for diverse perspectives, leaders can mitigate the risks of stagnation and unlock new levels of creativity and growth.

Translating Respect Equality Into Action

To ensure Respect Equality becomes more than just a concept, leaders must embrace actionable strategies. Here are three critical questions every leader can ask to bring this philosophy to life within their teams:

1. **How am I acknowledging the humanity of each team member today?**

   Demonstrate empathy and understanding by engaging with your team beyond their professional roles, recognizing their intrinsic worth as individuals.

2. **In what ways am I celebrating each team member's unique identities and contributions?**

   Create opportunities for team members to showcase their strengths, perspectives, and experiences, reinforcing their organizational value.

3. **What actions can I take today to promote inclusivity and belonging within my team?**

   Foster open communication, advocate for equitable policies, and challenge systemic barriers that hinder inclusivity.

These questions are reflective tools and a call to action for leaders at every level. By committing to human respect, leaders can transform their organizations into environments where individuals are empowered to thrive.

Fostering Inclusivity and Collaboration

When we prioritize human respect, we create environments where mutual empowerment becomes the norm. Instead of perceiving differences—whether based on gender, cultural background, or identity—as barriers, we learn to see them as assets that enrich our collective strength. By valuing the unique contributions of each individual, we unlock the full potential of our workplaces and society, fostering innovation, creativity, and progress.

Human respect is the cornerstone of inclusivity and collaboration. It fosters open dialogue, mutual understanding, and empathy, building the foundation for meaningful relationships and cross-gender partnerships. In such an environment, diverse talents and perspectives converge, leading to holistic and innovative solutions to the challenges we face. Inclusivity is not just an aspiration—it is a strategic advantage.

Leadership vs. Management:
A New Paradigm

As we delve deeper into the dynamics of fostering human respect, we must differentiate between the roles of leadership and management in shaping organizational culture. In today's rapidly evolving world, this distinction is pivotal.

Empowered leadership transcends traditional concepts of authority and control. It is not about issuing commands but about inspiring and enabling team members to achieve their full potential. Empowered leaders prioritize autonomy, creativity, and innovation over rigid oversight and micromanagement. They create an environment where individuals feel trusted, valued, and motivated to contribute their best.

At its core, empowered leadership shifts the focus from control to collaboration. Leaders act as enablers, offering guidance, support, and resources, trusting their teams to excel. This approach fosters a culture of trust, accountability, and shared ownership, where team members feel genuinely invested in the organization's success.

In contrast, traditional management often adheres to hierarchical structures and centralized control. Managers focus on planning, organizing, and executing tasks, ensuring compliance with established protocols and maintaining order. While these functions are critical for operational stability, they can inadvertently stifle creativity and innovation, particularly if they lean too heavily on rigidity.

A Call for Balance

The distinction between leadership and management is not a question of choosing one over the other but recognizing their complementary roles. While management provides structure and operational efficiency, empowered leadership drives growth, adaptability, and resilience. Together, they create the conditions for organizations to thrive in a complex and dynamic world.

In the context of the billion-dollar issue of disengagement and exclusion, empowered leadership stands as a solution. Leaders who embrace human respect and inclusivity foster environments where individuals feel seen, valued, and empowered to contribute. They break down silos, challenge biases, and cultivate collaboration, paving the way for sustained success going forward.

The Respect Equality Model calls us to embrace this balance—leveraging management's strengths while cultivating the transformative potential of empowered leadership. By doing so, we address the pressing challenges of the present and lay the foundation for a future defined by innovation, equity, and collective progress.

In the next section, we'll dive into how to use the Respect Equality Model to achieve concrete outcomes in the workplace.

PART 3

Using The Respect Equality Model To Navigate Workplace Challenges

The Human Advantage

The value of technology lies in its ability to augment human imagination and creativity.
—Simon Sinek

Following my accident, I questioned a great many things about my place in the working world. Most people won't experience such a traumatic event, but it's natural for humans to ask the same kind of questions. This is particularly true with the rapid advancement of technology and automation, which has led to uncertainty about where we fit in and what unique contributions we bring. On a deeper level, this shift has sparked a collective, often subconscious, questioning of what it truly means to be human in an artificial-intelligence-driven world.

What value do we, as individuals, bring to the table that cannot be replicated by algorithms?

These questions tie directly to our basic psychological needs for autonomy, competence, and belonging. As humans, everyone craves a sense of purpose, mastery, and connection—needs that are deeply interwoven with our professional lives. If not handled thoughtfully, integrating AI into workplaces risks destabilizing these core needs, potentially exacerbating what we've identified as the *Billion Dollar Blind Spot*: a crisis of disengagement, disconnection, and a lack of psychological safety within organizations. This issue has already manifested in poor workplace cultures, high employee turnover, and significant economic losses.

If implemented without attention to its human impact, technology can widen the divides we already see in society—between the empowered and the marginalized, the skilled and the displaced. Among the most pressing of these divides is the gender gap, which risks being perpetuated, and even exacerbated, by the potential biases embedded in many new artificial intelligence systems. As technology advances, those who feel left behind may retreat further into disconnection and disillusionment, intensifying workplace disengagement and deepening societal inequalities.

The issue lies in how the software is being built. Many systems are developed within the framework of the patriarchal system that has historically shaped societal norms, workplaces, and decision-making processes. These systems are often created by predominantly male teams, unintentionally encoding biases that reflect the existing inequalities in our society. For instance, algorithms designed to evaluate job candidates have been found to favor male applicants simply because they were trained on data from a male-dominated workforce. This perpetuates a cycle where women and gender-diverse individuals face additional barriers to entry and advancement.

This bias isn't just damaging for women—it also harms men by reinforcing outdated stereotypes. The patriarchal bias in automated systems can uphold rigid expectations for men to conform to stoic, emotionless leadership styles, further entrenching toxic masculinity and discouraging emotional mastery or vulnerability in the workplace. This creates a double-edged sword: while women continue to be excluded, men are boxed into roles that deny them the full range of human expression, stifling innovation and emotional intelligence.

When these systems replicate and amplify the biases of the patriarchal system, they do more than perpetuate existing inequalities; they normalize them, embedding these issues into the very fabric of how organizations operate. This threatens to deepen workplace disengagement by creating environments where women feel undervalued and excluded, and men feel trapped in narrow definitions of leadership and worth. Such systems also overlook the tremendous value that diverse teams bring to innovation and problem-solving, weakening organizations in the long term.

If we fail to address these biases, the artificial intelligence revolution will not only widen existing divides but also create new fault lines, eroding trust in both technology and leadership. Addressing this requires a conscious effort to build systems that challenge, rather than replicate, inequities. This means prioritizing diversity in the teams that develop the software, critically examining training data for inherent biases, and continuously auditing algorithms to ensure fair and equitable outcomes. It also means that companies which consider such systems need to be active participants in adopting the process, soliciting input from everyone on places where the software is reflecting or reinforcing unhelpful approaches. Remember that empowered leadership shifts the focus from control to collaboration.

By acknowledging and addressing these patriarchal biases, we have an opportunity to create systems that empower rather than exclude. In doing so, we can actually harness it as a force for equity, fostering workplaces where both men and women can thrive. This is not only a moral imperative but also a practical one—as we've noted, organizations that embrace diversity and emotional intelligence consistently outperform those that do not, highlighting that inclusivity is not just the right thing to do but the smart thing to do.

Artificial intelligence is a tool, and it can be used to amplify what makes us human. The answer in mindful integration of AI systems into the workplace lies not in resisting technology but in embracing emotional mastery and intentionally creating workplaces that value the human experience. Only then can we ensure that the systems enhance our shared sense of purpose and belonging rather than diminishes them.

It's crucial to recognize and embrace our human advantage, particularly in leadership roles. While machines excel at processing data and executing tasks precisely, they lack the nuanced understanding, empathy, and creativity innate to human beings. As leaders, it's essential to harness and leverage these uniquely human qualities to drive innovation, inspire teams, and navigate complex challenges, particularly in addressing the *Billion Dollar Blind Spot* of disengagement, disconnection, and lack of psychological safety.

There are several key human qualities that are indispensable in creating thriving, inclusive workplace cultures:

1. Empathy and Emotional Intelligence
   Example: Empathy allows leaders to truly understand the emotions and motivations of their teams, fostering a culture of psychological safety. For instance, a leader noticing signs of burnout in their team can initiate meaningful conversations and provide support— something an AI tool, no matter how advanced, cannot replicate. Emotional intelligence enables leaders to

navigate difficult conversations with grace, building trust and loyalty within their teams.

2. Creativity and Innovation
   Example: AI can analyze trends and generate ideas based on data, but it cannot ideate in the way humans can. Creative thinking thrives on diverse perspectives and the ability to connect seemingly unrelated concepts. A leader who cultivates an environment of collaboration can unlock innovative solutions to problems—like redesigning workplace processes to improve engagement—showcasing the kind of ingenuity that drives organizational success.

3. Ethical Judgement
   Example: AI operates within the parameters it is programmed with, but it lacks the ability to make value-based decisions. On the other hand, leaders can weigh complex ethical considerations, such as ensuring fairness in how AI systems are implemented in the workplace or addressing biases in hiring practices. This ethical discernment is critical for fostering trust and maintaining a strong organizational reputation.

4. Resilience and Adaptability
   Example: Humans excel at adapting to changing

circumstances and learning from setbacks, a quality essential in leadership. A leader navigating an organizational crisis—such as a sudden shift in market conditions or an unexpected failure—can rally their team, communicate effectively, and turn adversity into an opportunity for growth. This kind of resilience is what propels organizations forward during times of uncertainty.

5. Vision and Storytelling

   Example: While AI can process data and identify patterns, it cannot inspire people to follow a shared vision. Leaders who can articulate a compelling purpose and connect it to the personal values of their teams create alignment and motivation. For example, addressing the *Billion Dollar Blind Spot* requires strategies and a powerful narrative that emphasizes the importance of well-being, inclusion, and engagement.

6. Fostering Connection

   Example: One of the biggest challenges in workplaces today is the erosion of human connection, exacerbated by digital tools and automation. Leaders have the unique ability to create environments where individuals feel valued and connected. For instance, implementing team-building activities or creating open channels for feedback demonstrates the human touch that builds camaraderie and trust.

By focusing on these uniquely human qualities, leaders can position themselves and their organizations to survive and thrive in the age of AI. These attributes are critical in tackling the *Billion Dollar Blind Spot* because they directly address the root causes of disengagement and disconnection. Artificial intelligence may amplify efficiency, but it's the uniquely human qualities will drive meaningful innovation, strengthen workplace cultures, and ensure the long-term success of organizations in a rapidly evolving world.

One powerful tool that makes us uniquely human is the concept of **mental models**—our internal algorithms for understanding and navigating the world. Mental models are frameworks we develop based on experience, knowledge, and perception, helping us interpret information, make decisions, and predict outcomes. Unlike algorithms, which are programmed and static unless updated, our mental models are dynamic, evolving through learning, reflection, and adaptation. They enable us to apply abstract thinking, recognize patterns in unfamiliar situations, and integrate emotional and ethical considerations into our decisions, giving us a significant edge in solving complex, nuanced challenges.

Think of mental models as the unseen structures beneath the surface of our conscious awareness, shaping our thoughts, beliefs, and actions. Like an iceberg, much of our mental activity lies beneath the surface, influencing our perceptions and decisions without our explicit awareness.

By embracing the iceberg model, we can delve beneath the surface of our thoughts and experiences, uncovering the patterns and structures that drive our behavior. This deeper understanding allows us to recognize and challenge unhelpful patterns, biases, and assumptions that may limit our potential as leaders.

Consider the Ladder of Inference we discussed earlier. It offers valuable insights into how our thoughts and actions are formulated. This framework highlights how we select, interpret, and act upon information, illustrating the interconnectedness of our beliefs, experiences, and actions. It provides a structured understanding of how seemingly automatic, deeper cognitive and emotional processes shape responses.

For leadership, the Ladder of Inference is particularly relevant because it uncovers the often-unseen biases and assumptions that influence decision-making. By recognizing how we move from observing raw data to taking action, leaders can become more self-aware and deliberate in their choices. This self-awareness is a cornerstone of emotional mastery and critical for creating workplace cultures that value psychological safety and inclusivity. For example, leaders who understand how their assumptions impact their decisions can pause to question whether their interpretations are accurate or whether personal biases unconsciously influence them.

In the context of the *Billion Dollar Blind Spot*—characterized by disengagement, disconnection, and toxic environments—the ladder of inference provides a tool for addressing these challenges. Leaders equipped with this framework can better navigate complex interpersonal dynamics by identifying and addressing the root causes of conflict or misunderstanding. It helps them foster trust and collaboration by ensuring their actions are aligned with their values and organizational goals.

Mental models such as the ladder of inference provide us with uniquely human insight into the complex interplay between our perceptions, beliefs, and actions. This awareness allows us to recognize and challenge unhelpful thinking patterns, question our assumptions, and consider alternative perspectives. Ultimately, by climbing down the ladder and examining our thought processes with intentionality and self-awareness, we can make more informed decisions, foster deeper understanding, and cultivate thriving leadership practices.

Emotional Mastery:
The Key to Resilient Leadership

In a world where leaders are often swept up in a whirlwind of demands and conflicting priorities, the ability to navigate emotions with clarity and purpose is more than a desirable trait—it's essential. Emotional mastery is the foundation of effective leadership, allowing individuals to rise above reactive impulses and align their thoughts and actions with their values and objectives. As described by leading psychologists such as Paul Ekman and Daniel Goleman, emotions are not barriers to effective decision-making but integral elements of the human experience that must be understood and channeled constructively. When leaders suppress or disassociate from their emotions, they risk letting those unprocessed feelings unconsciously drive their thoughts and actions, creating a disconnect between their intent and impact.

Stoicism and the Influence of Emotions on Leadership

Stoicism, often mischaracterized as emotional suppression or detachment, is in fact a philosophy that calls for a profound engagement with our emotional landscape. True stoicism is about achieving emotional mastery—not by ignoring or stifling emotions, but by recognizing, understanding, and integrating them in ways that align with our values and intentions. This deeper approach acknowledges that when unexamined or suppressed, emotions do not disappear; they operate unconsciously, shaping our perceptions, decisions, and behaviors.

Leaders who embrace stoicism in its authentic form gain the ability to navigate their inner world with clarity and purpose, transforming their emotions into deliberate actions rather than reactive impulses. This mastery bridges the gap between intent and impact, allowing leaders to foster trust, resilience, and alignment within their teams and organizations.

Suppressed Emotions and the Ladder of Inference

When emotions are suppressed or dissociated from, they do not disappear. Instead, they operate beneath the surface, influencing thoughts, perceptions, and behaviors in ways that individuals may not consciously recognize. Suppression creates an emotional undercurrent that subtly informs each rung of the ladder of inference, driving actions that often feel logical but are deeply rooted in unresolved emotional experiences. Psychologists such as Brené Brown, who focuses on vulnerability, and Susan David, who explores emotional agility, highlight how unacknowledged emotions shape behavior and decision-making.

For example:

1. **Observation**: Suppressed emotions can act as filters, determining what information individuals pay attention to. A leader suppressing anxiety may unconsciously seek out data that validates a need for control or reinforces fears, even while consciously striving for objectivity.
2. **Selection**: Dissociated emotions influence what data is deemed relevant. A suppressed feeling of inadequacy might lead to overemphasis on information that confirms existing biases or decisions, avoiding data that challenges one's competence.
3. **Interpretation**: Emotions—whether acknowledged or not—color how individuals assign meaning to observations. For instance, unprocessed anger might lead a leader to interpret a colleague's neutral comment as criticism.
4. **Action**: The culmination of these unconscious processes drives behaviors. Often rationalized as logical, actions are reactions to the emotional undercurrent, potentially misaligned with organizational values or objectives.

The Role of Emotional Awareness in Leadership

Psychologists like Susan David advocate for emotional agility—the ability to confront emotions with curiosity and compassion, rather than avoidance. Emotional agility enables leaders to integrate emotions into the decision-making process in a constructive way. Conversely, suppression denies this integration, leading to actions disconnected from personal values or organizational goals.

Brené Brown further underscores the importance of vulnerability in leadership. Embracing vulnerability involves acknowledging emotions rather than suppressing them. This fosters deeper self-awareness and authenticity, creating a leadership style that inspires trust and psychological safety.

Practical Steps for Emotional Mastery in Leadership

To avoid the pitfalls of suppression or dissociation, leaders can take steps to engage with their emotions constructively:

1. **Cultivate Self-Awareness**: Regularly reflect on emotional triggers and patterns. Practices like mindfulness

and journaling can help leaders identify suppressed emotions.

2. **Practice Emotional Agility**: Confront emotions with curiosity, seeking to understand their origins and influence. This aligns with Susan David's approach to emotional agility as a means to enhance decision-making.

3. **Adopt Stoic Practices**: True stoicism involves pausing to evaluate emotional responses and aligning actions with long-term values and objectives, rather than immediate emotional impulses.

4. **Seek Feedback**: Encourage honest feedback from peers and teams to uncover blind spots created by unacknowledged emotions.

By integrating these practices, leaders can embody the essence of true stoicism, navigating the ladder of inference with emotional awareness and intentionality. This approach strengthens decision-making and cultivates a leadership style that is authentic, inclusive, and inspiring. Through understanding and mastering emotions—not suppressing them—leaders can drive meaningful, value-aligned actions in their organizations.

The Human Solution to the Billion Dollar Problem

Workplaces that fail to prioritize human psychological well-being are at the heart of this issue. Cultures of fear, suppression, and disengagement are detrimental to individuals and financially unsustainable. According to Gallup, disengaged employees cost the global economy trillions annually, and Beyond Blue's findings show how workplace-related mental health issues impose billions in costs on Australian employers alone.

Layering the AI revolution onto this already fragile foundation creates a volatile situation. Management's eager embrace of AI's capabilities in decision-making, efficiency, and automation may inadvertently lead to feelings of redundancy, loss of purpose, and heightened anxiety among employees. The human response to these technological shifts often manifests emotionally, making it more critical than ever for leaders to cultivate emotional mastery to navigate the turbulence.

How Emotional Mastery Addresses These Challenges

Emotional mastery is the key to transforming workplace cultures and mitigating the psychological and organizational costs exacerbated by AI integration. By understanding and managing emotions—both personal and within teams—leaders can create environments where people feel valued, resilient, and connected, keeping an eye on the Respect Equality Equation. This focus is the key to understanding how emotional mastery can be used constructively in the workplace.

Mapping the Issues to Solutions Through Emotional Mastery

1. **Disengagement and Low Morale**:
   - **Issue**: AI can inadvertently depersonalize work, making employees feel undervalued or replaceable.
   - **Solution**: Leaders with emotional mastery can counteract this by fostering human-centric environments. By recognizing and addressing feelings of disconnection, they can create a sense of belonging and purpose, leveraging Goleman's principles of emotional intelligence to re-engage employees.

2. **Resistance to Change**:
   - **Issue**: Introducing AI can spark fear and resistance, often rooted in unacknowledged emotions such as inadequacy or uncertainty.
   - **Solution**: Leaders can model resilience and optimism through self-awareness and emotional regulation.

They can help teams navigate these changes empathetically, ensuring open dialogue and reducing fear.

3. **Psychological Safety**:
   - **Issue**: Poor workplace cultures discourage vulnerability, leaving employees hesitant to express concerns or innovate.
   - **Solution**: Emotional mastery enables leaders to create safe spaces for dialogue. Brené Brown's work on vulnerability highlights that emotionally intelligent leaders foster trust and innovation, critical in navigating the complexities of AI-driven change.

4. **Impact on Mental Health**:
   - **Issue**: Suppressed emotions and fear of obsolescence can exacerbate anxiety and stress in an AI-driven workplace.
   - **Solution**: Leaders grounded in stoic principles, as emphasized by Donald Robertson, can inspire calm and focus amid uncertainty. They can reduce stress and cultivate resilience by validating employees' emotions and aligning actions with core organizational values.

The Human Need for Emotional Mastery in an AI-Driven World

In San Francisco, I saw an advertising campaign boldly declared, "Stop hiring humans—the era of AI employees is here." The campaign, which touted the benefits of artificial intelligence over human labor, provocatively suggested, "AI artisans won't complain about work-life balance." This message struck a nerve with me, not just as a business leader but as a CPA, where I've long grappled with how we account for people on the balance sheet. Labelling humans as "expenses" and "liabilities" has always irked me—our workforce is our greatest asset, not a cost to be minimized. It's an asset that requires thoughtful investment, development, and care.

This ad campaign's stark rhetoric highlights a disturbing trend of devaluing the human contribution in favor of AI's perceived perfection. But here's the truth: no algorithm can replace the creativity, empathy, and resilience that humans bring to the table. As leaders, it's our responsibility to challenge this mindset. We must invest in our people, not only because it's ethically right but because the long-term success of any business depends on the growth and well-being of its greatest asset—its people. AI should augment human potential, not render it obsolete. The narrative must shift, starting with how we perceive and prioritize our workforce. Disengagement, disconnection, and the erosion of psychological safety are not just challenges—they are opportunities to reimagine workplaces that amplify human creativity, empathy, and collaboration.

The path forward begins with self-awareness. As you explore this book, reflect on your mental models and the unseen forces shaping your decisions.

Leveraging the Power of Masculinity

*A hero is someone who has give his or
her life to something bigger than oneself.*
—Joseph Campbell.

My path towards the Respect Equality Equation led me to reconsider many aspects of workplace culture and my own professional identity, including traditionally masculine traits.

In the ever-evolving leadership landscape, the concept of masculinity holds a profound significance. Historically shaped by societal norms and expectations, traditional masculinity has long been associated with qualities such as stoicism, dominance, and emotional suppression. While these traits were once heralded as essential for success and survival, their narrow scope has become increasingly misaligned with the demands of modern leadership and human well-being.

As we navigate an era defined by technological

advancements and a deeper understanding of human psychology, it is clear that clinging to outdated definitions of masculinity is not only limiting but also harmful. The relentless pressure to conform to rigid gender norms has led to a cascade of psychological challenges, including emotional repression, social isolation, and strained relationships. The inability to process emotions healthily often results in anxiety, depression, and a pervasive sense of disconnection—not just from others but also from oneself.

Amidst these challenges lies a transformative opportunity: the emergence of **inclusive masculinity.** Defined by traits such as empathy, vulnerability, and collaboration, this evolved understanding of masculinity marks a paradigm shift. It rejects the false notion that strength is synonymous with emotional detachment or dominance and instead embraces emotional intelligence as the cornerstone of true resilience and leadership.

Emotional mastery is central to this shift—the ability to constructively understand, regulate, and channel emotions. Emotional mastery is not about suppressing emotions but recognizing their presence, understanding their origins, and using them to guide thoughtful action. For men, cultivating this skill means breaking free from the constraints of traditional masculinity and fostering a healthier relationship with their inner selves.

Emotional mastery serves as a powerful antidote to

the psychological ill-being that stems from emotional suppression. By learning to process emotions effectively, men can reduce the risk of internalizing stress or resorting to maladaptive coping mechanisms such as aggression or withdrawal. This enhances personal well-being and strengthens interpersonal relationships, enabling men to lead with authenticity and empathy.

Moreover, inclusive masculinity and emotional mastery align closely with modern leadership principles. Leaders who embody these qualities inspire trust, foster collaboration, and create psychologically safe environments where their teams can thrive. When leaders demonstrate vulnerability, they model courage and authenticity, encouraging others to bring their full selves to work. When they prioritize empathy, they build bridges of understanding that transcend differences, fostering a sense of belonging and collective purpose.

Ultimately, the shift from traditional to inclusive masculinity needs to be a societal evolution and is a critical component of leadership transformation. Emotional mastery empowers men to navigate the complexities of modern life with resilience and purpose, enabling them to lead themselves and others toward healthier, more fulfilling futures. True strength lies not in denying our emotions, but in harnessing them to build deeper connections and drive meaningful change.

The Turning Point:
From Suppression to Strength

Before my life-altering horse-riding accident, I was entrenched in a traditional masculine mindset, one that prized stoicism, emotional suppression, and an unwavering focus on pushing my mind and body to their limits. As a competitive dressage rider striving for excellence at the highest levels, I often found myself compartmentalizing emotions, viewing vulnerability as a weakness to be avoided at all costs. While seemingly effective in pursuit of athletic success, this approach left me feeling isolated and disconnected from those around me. Despite outward appearances of strength and determination, I grappled with a profound sense of loneliness, struggling to forge meaningful connections with others.

However, the moment my life was irrevocably altered by the accident, I was forced to confront the limitations of this rigid masculine paradigm. Suddenly thrust into a reality where my body and dreams lay shattered, I found myself standing at a crossroads—with the choice between succumbing to despair or embracing a new, more inclusive way of being. In that crucible of adversity, I discovered the transformative power of vulnerability, empathy, and self-compassion. Moving from suppression to emotional mastery, I began to understand that true strength lies not in denying emotions but in owning and mastering them. This shift unlocked an inner resilience, empowering me to face challenges with clarity and grace while building deeper connections with those around me.

To navigate the arduous journey of recovery and rehabilitation, I was faced with a pivotal choice: to adopt the mindset of a victim or a victor. Challenges, whether physical, emotional, or situational, knock on all of our doors, and our response defines the path forward. For me, this meant shedding the armor of emotional detachment and confronting the profound grief, fear, and uncertainty that came with my shattered reality.

This choice required unwavering self-leadership—the ability to take control of my mindset and actions despite the overwhelming odds. It was a journey marked by profound self-reflection, where I had to confront my vulnerabilities and extend kindness and understanding to myself amidst immense physical and emotional pain. In those moments, I realized that the impossible could only become possible through the mastery of my emotions.

True strength, I discovered, is not in suppressing emotions but in the courage to embrace and master them. Emotional mastery is not about eliminating fear or pain; it is about understanding, channeling, and using them as fuel for growth. By embracing vulnerability as a source of strength rather than weakness, I unlocked the ability to forge deeper, more authentic connections with my medical team, my loved ones, and, most importantly, myself.

This transformation was about healing my body and redefining how I approached life's challenges. It showed me that self-leadership and emotional mastery are the key to turning adversity into opportunity and the impossible into a tangible reality.

This personal transformation fundamentally altered my approach to leadership, both of myself and others. No longer bound by the constraints of traditional masculinity, I discovered the liberating power of curiosity, vulnerability, and empathy in navigating life's challenges and inspiring meaningful change. Today, I stand as living proof that embracing our humanity—in all its complexity and imperfection—is the key to personal resilience and growth and the foundation of truly impactful leadership.

To navigate this landscape effectively, it's essential to establish a common understanding of key concepts that shape our discourse on gender. Drawing from academic research and scholarly discourse, we delve into the definitions of masculine mindset, feminine mindset, and movements which have stemmed from and in reaction to each.

In navigating the dialogue surrounding masculinity, addressing the terminology used to describe these societal norms and expectations is crucial. While acknowledging the potentially detrimental effects of traditional masculine archetypes (often referred to as 'toxic' masculinity) on both individual well-being and organizational culture, I harbor a strong aversion to the term 'toxic masculinity'. This phrase, while attempting to highlight the harmful aspects of traditional masculinity, often inadvertently frames men as inherently toxic—an assertion I find deeply problematic. As we travel the path of personal and collective transformation in the face of technological advancement and societal evolution, it's imperative to recognize men's essential role in shaping our world.

Toxic masculinity is certainly a component of the billion-dollar problem. But it's important not to throw the figurative baby out with the bathwater. Rather than vilifying masculinity as inherently toxic, I advocate a more nuanced approach—one that acknowledges the harmful effects of traditional gender norms while empowering men to embrace a more inclusive form of masculinity. Now, more than ever, is the time for men to transcend the confines of traditional expectations and cultivate an ethos of inclusivity, empathy, and collaboration. As we strive to redefine masculinity in the modern era, let us move forward with a shared commitment to creating a world where all individuals, regardless of gender, can thrive and contribute to the collective flourishing of humanity.

History of Masculinity

Throughout history, the concept of masculinity has been shaped by various influences, from early societal structures to modern economic systems. In hunter-gatherer societies, roles were often defined by necessity rather than strict gender lines. However, with the advent of agrarian societies, property ownership and inheritance systems began favoring male lineage, laying the groundwork for patriarchal structures.

In ancient civilizations like Greece and Rome, masculinity was associated with traits like strength, honor, and stoicism, setting early models for Western notions of manhood. The Middle Ages feudal system further reinforced the link between masculinity and roles like land ownership and military service.

The Industrial Revolution was a transformative period that reshaped the fabric of society, fundamentally altering how men and women engaged with work, family, and each other. As factories rose and urbanization spread, the very structure of daily life changed, cementing a division of labor along gender lines that would have lasting implications on gender dynamics and the concept of masculinity.

The Disconnection from Emotional Mastery

Stoicism, as we've seen, is a philosophy traditionally about emotional mastery, not suppression. So what happened to change things? Prior to the Industrial Revolution, men often worked in agrarian or craft-based settings, where work and family life were closely intertwined. Fathers and sons worked side by side, and emotional bonds were naturally fostered through shared labor and the rhythm of daily life. This integration allowed men to express a broader range of emotions, particularly as mentors and caregivers within the family unit.

However, with the advent of industrialization, men were increasingly pulled into the public sphere, working long hours in factories under demanding and often dehumanizing conditions. Emotional expression, once integral to familial and community life, became a liability in industrial work's harsh, productivity-driven environment. The emphasis shifted toward emotional suppression, survival, and efficiency, qualities that were deemed essential for "thriving" in this new industrial landscape. Emotional mastery, once a hallmark of balanced leadership and familial connection, was replaced by emotional suppression—a necessity for enduring factory life's physical and psychological toll.

The Gender Divide

The division of labor during this period was stark: men became breadwinners, their value tied to economic productivity in the public sphere, while women were relegated to the domestic sphere, responsible for nurturing and managing the household. This dichotomy reinforced gender stereotypes that persist to this day. Men were expected to embody strength, control, and rationality, while women were cast as emotional caregivers, the keepers of warmth and empathy.

This separation served a practical purpose in the context of industrialization: it allowed families to function as economic units where each member had a clearly defined role. However, it also entrenched a gender divide that created significant barriers to emotional and psychological well-being. Men were disconnected from the nurturing aspects of life and discouraged from seeking or expressing emotional support, while women's contributions were undervalued, confined to unpaid and often invisible labor.

The Purpose Behind the Divide

The redefined gender divide was not an accidental byproduct of industrialization; it was a calculated adaptation to the demands of a rapidly changing economy and, perhaps more provocatively, a deliberate mechanism to bind men and women to their designated roles. By assigning men the role of worker and women the role of caretaker, the emerging industrial capitalist system ensured efficiency and specialization and a hierarchical order that served those at the top—the industrialists, landowners, and burgeoning capitalist elite.

This model effectively enslaved men and women into rigid gender roles, stripping them of autonomy and reducing their worth to their economic and reproductive utility. Men were tied to the factory floor, valued solely for their capacity to produce, while women were confined to the domestic sphere, their worth tied to their ability to sustain the family unit. The true beneficiaries of this system were not the workers or their families but the owners and overseers who profited immensely from this neatly divided labor system.

Who Benefited and Why

If the new system was rigid and led to a narrower and more unhealthy definition of gender roles, why was it adopted? The short answer is money. The capitalist elite reaped the rewards of this gendered division of labor in several keyways:

1. **Maximized Productivity:** By designating men as the breadwinners, the industrial system ensured a steady supply of workers who were willing to endure grueling hours and harsh conditions. The promise of supporting a family acted as a powerful motivator, even as wages remained low and working conditions perilous.

2. **Control over Labor:** Women's relegation to the domestic sphere ensured the stability of the workforce. By placing the burden of caregiving and homemaking on women, the system reduced demands on employers to provide childcare or family support, shifting those responsibilities entirely onto families.

3. **Economic Dependency:** The gender divide created a structure of economic dependency. Women, barred from earning comparable wages or entering the public workforce in significant numbers, became reliant on male income, further entrenching patriarchal power dynamics.

4. **Perpetuation of Class Hierarchies:** By keeping both genders confined to their roles, the industrial system ensured that neither men nor women could challenge the broader power structure. Men were too consumed with survival and providing for their families, while women were systematically excluded from spheres of influence.

Evidence of Intent

Historical records and economic analyses suggest that this divide was far from coincidental. In his seminal work *The Condition of the Working Class in England* (1845), Friedrich Engels described how industrialization exploited workers, particularly men, by turning them into mere cogs in a profit-driven machine. Simultaneously, the cult of domesticity, as highlighted by historians like Barbara Welter, placed women in a "separate sphere" of home and morality, reinforcing their subjugation.

The writings of 19th-century industrialists further illustrate this deliberate orchestration. Factory owners and policymakers actively supported gendered labor norms, recognizing that maintaining a patriarchal family structure would keep the workforce docile and compliant. For instance, arguments in favor of child labor laws often framed women's domesticity as essential for the moral development of future workers—a guise that obscured the economic benefits of free or low-cost caregiving.

The Cost of Gendered Enslavement

While the capitalist elite flourished, the costs for the broader population were immense:

- **Men:** Dehumanized and valued only for their ability to toil, men became emotionally isolated, with no room to express vulnerability or seek fulfilment beyond work. This disconnection set the stage for generational cycles of suppressed emotions and strained relationships.
- **Women:** Barred from economic independence, women were trapped in lives of unpaid labor, often invisible and unrecognized, even as their work underpinned the success of the industrial capitalist system.
- **Society:** By entrenching rigid gender roles, the system stifled innovation and collaboration. Half the population was excluded from intellectual and economic contributions, slowing societal progress and exacerbating inequality.

Breaking the Chains

Understanding this history is essential for dismantling its lingering effects. The industrial-era gender divide was not simply a reflection of its time but a calculated system of control and exploitation, one which has morphed over time into a billion-dollar problem. Recognizing this allows us to challenge its remnants in modern workplaces and relationships, advocating for systems that value all paid and unpaid contributions and create space for individuals to transcend traditional roles.

The next step in this journey is fostering emotional mastery and inclusivity, enabling men and women alike to reclaim their identities and contribute to a more equitable, thriving society.

Effects on Modern Masculinity

The legacy of the Industrial Revolution continues to shape modern masculinity. The emphasis on emotional suppression and economic productivity as measures of a man's worth has created a culture where vulnerability and emotional expression are often seen as weaknesses. Men are frequently socialized to prioritize success and control over connection and self-awareness, perpetuating cycles of emotional repression and isolation.

Moreover, the rigid roles established during the Industrial Revolution have contributed to ongoing gender inequality. While strides have been made toward gender equity, the remnants of this historical division linger in the workplace and home. Men are often expected to prioritize their careers over family life, while women continue to bear the brunt of caregiving responsibilities.

The time has come to break free from this legacy. Modern masculinity must evolve to embrace emotional mastery, vulnerability, and connection. This shift requires rejecting the outdated notion that men must sacrifice their mental health and personal lives to meet societal expectations. Instead, we must reframe vulnerability as a strength and emotional intelligence as a hallmark of true leadership.

Men need to be empowered to define their worth beyond their economic output. This involves fostering environments—in workplaces, homes, and communities—where emotional expression is celebrated, not stigmatized. Emotional mastery, the ability to recognize, process, and express emotions, is critical for individual well-being and building healthier relationships and more inclusive workplaces.

Redefining masculinity is not just a challenge for men but a societal imperative. Organizations must create cultures where men feel safe to step beyond traditional roles and engage fully as human beings. Leaders must model this behavior, demonstrating that emotional intelligence and collaboration are as valuable as competence and control. At the same time, societal norms must shift to value caregiving and domestic contributions equally, enabling both men and women to participate fully in all aspects of life.

Traditional Masculinity

To move past traditional masculinity, often referred to as 'toxic' masculinity, it's necessary to understand it. It's a set of rigid and harmful norms and expectations placed on men that prioritize traits such as dominance, aggression, emotional suppression, and the pursuit of power and control. Traditional masculinity can perpetuate harmful behaviors and attitudes that not only harm men themselves but also contribute to the oppression and marginalization of women and other marginalized genders

Traditional masculinity is characterized by the belief that men must conform to narrow and unrealistic standards of behavior in order to prove their manhood. This can manifest in various ways, including:

Emotional Suppression vs. Emotional Mastery

1. Emotional Suppression:

Traditional masculinity often demands conformity to norms that discourage men from expressing vulnerability, sensitivity, or emotions other than anger. From an early age, boys are socialized to equate emotional expression with weakness or inadequacy, reinforcing the harmful notion that vulnerability is inherently "feminine" and, therefore, undesirable. Phrases like *"Boys don't cry"* echo through generations, implying that stoicism and emotional restraint are marks of strength and maturity.

This conditioning leads to a cycle of emotional suppression where men learn to bury their feelings rather than confront or process them. Suppressing emotions does not make them disappear; instead, it internalizes stress, leading to chronic mental and physical health issues such as anxiety, depression, and cardiovascular problems. Additionally, emotional suppression hinders authentic connections with others, fostering isolation and making it difficult for men to build meaningful relationships, including in the workplace.

2. Emotional Mastery:

In contrast, emotional mastery is about recognizing, understanding, and managing one's emotions constructively. It is not about abandoning control or indulging in every fleeting feeling but rather about cultivating emotional intelligence—the ability to navigate emotions with self-awareness and purpose. Emotional mastery transforms vulnerability from a perceived weakness into a profound strength. It allows men to face challenges head-on, not by suppressing their emotions but by acknowledging and harnessing them.

Emotional mastery involves learning to:

- **Identify emotions:** Recognizing what you feel and why.
- **Process emotions:** Understanding the root causes and

effects of emotions, rather than dismissing or ignoring them.

- **Communicate effectively:** Expressing emotions constructively, which enhances relationships and fosters trust.
- **Regulate responses:** Maintaining composure in difficult situations without suppressing emotional truths.

Unlike suppression, which isolates individuals from their humanity, emotional mastery fosters resilience, adaptability, and growth. It enables men to approach adversity with clarity and strength, connecting their inner world to their external actions in a way that drives personal and professional success.

The Costs of Suppression and the Power of Mastery

The societal emphasis on emotional suppression has created a culture where anger often becomes the only "acceptable" outlet for men's feelings. This narrow emotional bandwidth can lead to misplaced aggression, perpetuating cycles of frustration and conflict. By contrast, emotional mastery offers men the tools to engage with their full spectrum of emotions, breaking free from the constraints of traditional gender norms.

Men who embrace emotional mastery improve their mental and physical well-being and elevate their leadership capabilities. They are better equipped to foster psychological safety within teams, inspire trust, and drive meaningful change. Emotional mastery is a cornerstone of modern masculinity, demonstrating that true strength lies in understanding and leveraging emotions—not in denying their existence.

Dominance and Aggression:
The Glorification of Power and Control

Traditional masculinity also venerates traits like dominance, aggression, and physical strength, framing them as essential markers of a "real man." Men are socialized to believe that asserting power and control—whether through competition, coercion, or physical prowess—is the ultimate expression of masculinity. This mindset is reinforced by societal narratives that valorize dominance as strength and aggression as decisive action.

While these traits may have been advantageous in historical contexts where physical survival depended on displays of power, their glorification in modern society often comes at a significant cost, both psychologically and economically.

Psychological Effects

1. **Erosion of Mental Health:**
   Men conditioned to prioritize dominance and aggression often struggle with repressed emotions and unresolved conflicts. This internal battle can lead to anxiety, depression, and anger management issues, as the constant pressure to assert control leaves little room for vulnerability or emotional expression. Research highlights that men adhering to these norms are less likely to seek help for mental health struggles, exacerbating feelings of isolation and emotional distress.

2. **Toxic Relationships:**
   Dominance as a behavioral standard often leads to strained personal and professional relationships. Men who view power as a zero-sum game may struggle to collaborate, empathize, or form meaningful connections, resulting in a cycle of mistrust and conflict. In romantic and family dynamics, this can escalate to controlling or abusive behaviors, further perpetuating cycles of harm.

3. **Imposter Syndrome and Insecurity:**
   The pressure to consistently project strength and control creates a fragile sense of self-worth, as any

perceived weakness feels like a failure of masculinity. Men caught in this paradigm may mask their insecurities with outward aggression, leading to a disconnect between their internal struggles and external behaviors.

Economic Effects

1. **Workplace Conflict and Reduced Productivity:**
   Dominance-driven behaviors in the workplace often create toxic environments, marked by competition instead of collaboration. Aggressive leadership styles can stifle innovation, discourage open dialogue, and increase employee turnover.

2. **Barrier to Inclusive Leadership:**
   The emphasis on dominance often excludes traits like empathy, collaboration, and adaptability qualities essential for effective leadership in today's dynamic, diverse workplaces. This perpetuates outdated hierarchies that hinder organizational progress and exclude talent from underrepresented groups.

3. **Economic Cost of Violence:**
   The societal glorification of aggression contributes to broader issues like domestic violence, workplace bullying, and even criminal behavior. The World

Health Organization estimates that gender-based violence alone costs global economies trillions annually.

A Shift Toward Balance

The overemphasis on dominance and aggression fails to acknowledge the complexity and multifaceted nature of masculine strength. True resilience and leadership come not from controlling others but from empowering them, a principle that runs counter to traditional masculine ideals. By shifting focus from dominance to collaboration and from aggression to emotional intelligence, men can foster environments that prioritize psychological well-being, enhance economic performance, and support personal growth.

Rejecting the glorification of dominance does not mean rejecting masculinity; it means redefining strength as the ability to lead with empathy, create with humility, and connect with authenticity. This evolution is critical for individual well-being and essential for building equitable and thriving communities and economies.

Sexual Objectification:
Reducing Others to Conquest

Traditional masculinity also frequently ties a man's worth to his sexual prowess, promoting the idea that power, status, and validation are achieved through the conquest of women and, by extension, the objectification of non-binary individuals. This mindset is deeply embedded in societal narratives, media portrayals, and cultural expectations, normalizing the reduction of others to mere objects of desire or achievement.

This harmful framework perpetuates inequities and generates significant psychological and economic consequences for individuals and society.

Psychological Effects

1. **Erosion of Healthy Relationships:**
   When traditional masculinity emphasizes conquest over connection, it undermines the ability to form meaningful, respectful relationships. Men who internalize this mindset may struggle with intimacy, empathy, and mutual respect, creating dynamics that lack depth and authenticity. Over time, this hinders their ability to build fulfilling and equitable partnerships.

2. **Internalized Insecurity:**
   By equating self-worth with sexual conquests, men often develop a fragile sense of masculinity tied to external validation. This creates a cycle of insecurity, as each conquest becomes a fleeting attempt to affirm

their value, leaving them emotionally disconnected and perpetually seeking more.

3. **Reinforcement of Harmful Gender Norms:**
Sexual objectification dehumanizes women and non-binary individuals, reducing them to roles that exist solely to validate male egos. This dynamic perpetuates feelings of disempowerment and devaluation in those who are objectified, contributing to widespread societal harm.

Economic Effects

1. **Workplace Harassment and Legal Costs:**
The objectification of others often manifests in workplace dynamics, leading to harassment, discrimination, and toxic environments. The Equality and Human Rights Commission estimates that sexual harassment costs organizations millions annually in lost economic potential.

2. **Impact on Career Advancement:**
Objectification often contributes to systemic barriers that hinder the advancement of women and non-binary individuals in professional spaces. When individuals are seen through a lens of objectification rather than capability, their contributions are undervalued, leading

to missed opportunities for organizations to harness diverse talents and perspectives.

3. **Economic Inequality:**
The perpetuation of traditional masculinity in the form of sexual objectification reinforces gender pay gaps and unequal opportunities. By undermining the credibility and capabilities of objectified individuals, the system sustains economic disparities that hinder societal progress.

A Shift Toward Respectful Connection

Rejecting the sexual objectification embedded in traditional masculinity is about fostering an ethos of respect and recognizing the inherent dignity of all individuals. True masculinity involves cultivating meaningful relationships based on equality, consent, and authenticity rather than conquest and control.

To achieve this, men must:

1. **Embrace Emotional Mastery:** Cultivate the ability to understand and regulate emotions, replacing the need for external validation with internal self-worth.
2. **Champion Equality:** Advocate for inclusive spaces where everyone is valued for their talents and contributions, not their appearance or perceived desirability.

3. **Redefine Success:** Shift away from conquest-based definitions of masculinity toward measures of success grounded in empathy, connection, and collaboration.

The Path Forward

Addressing the culture of sexual objectification requires systemic change and individual accountability. By dismantling the harmful norms of traditional masculinity and embracing a model of respect and equality, society can foster healthier interpersonal dynamics, equitable professional environments, and greater economic potential.

Empowering men to move beyond conquest toward authentic connection benefits everyone. It promotes psychological well-being, strengthens societal bonds, and unlocks the full potential of diverse perspectives and contributions—a win for individuals, organizations, and society as a whole.

Breaking the Chains of Emotional Suppression

The men I've interviewed often describe feeling trapped by traditional norms dictating how they are 'allowed' to behave. These norms frequently lead to emotional repression, isolation, and strained relationships, resulting in cycles of stress, anxiety, and even aggression—the one emotion society deems acceptable for men to express. The consequences ripple beyond the individual, affecting teams, organizations, and society as a whole.

One vivid example came from a conversation I had on a construction site. A male worker aggressively voiced opposition to women working there, initially framing his argument as a matter of capability and safety. "Women have no place here," he said. "This is dangerous work, and they just can't handle it." His tone suggested deeply ingrained bias, but rather than reacting defensively, I engaged him with curiosity.

As the conversation progressed, it became evident that his aggression masked a profound fear of inadequacy. He felt an overwhelming sense of responsibility to protect his colleagues, particularly women, and worried that he might fail to meet those expectations. This fear, rooted in traditional masculine norms, had left him anxious and defensive, unable to articulate his concerns constructively.

I saw a transformation by addressing his fears directly and reframing the narrative around shared responsibility and teamwork. He began to acknowledge the professionalism and competence of his female colleagues, shifting from opposition to advocacy. "I never thought about it that way," he admitted. "We all need to support each other."

This moment highlighted the power of emotional mastery—recognizing and addressing the underlying emotions driving behavior rather than reacting to surface-level aggression. It also reinforced the importance of psychological safety: creating spaces where individuals feel safe to express vulnerability and explore deeper emotions without fear of judgment.

Linking Themes to Action

Traditional masculinity's emphasis on dominance and suppression doesn't just harm men; it also undermines organizational culture by stifling collaboration, trust, and innovation. Leaders play a crucial role in dismantling these norms and fostering cultures of inclusivity and psychological safety.

Actionable Steps for Leaders:

1. **Promote Emotional Literacy:** Equip teams with tools to constructively recognize, articulate, and manage emotions. This reduces conflict and builds stronger interpersonal connections.
2. **Create Safe Spaces:** Encourage open dialogue and model vulnerability to show that expressing emotions isn't a sign of weakness but a path to strength.
3. **Address Root Causes:** Recognize that aggression or resistance often stems from fear or insecurity. Engage with empathy to uncover and resolve underlying concerns.

Leaders can drive meaningful cultural change by cultivating environments where emotional mastery replaces suppression. This benefits individuals and strengthens teams, enhancing organizational resilience and performance. True leadership lies in empowering others to move beyond traditional norms, embracing emotional intelligence and collaboration to build cultures where everyone can thrive.

Inclusive Masculinity:
A Blueprint for Transforming the Workplace

Inclusive Masculinity offers a modern, transformative approach to manhood that moves beyond traditional norms of dominance, stoicism, and emotional suppression. It embraces respect, equality, and emotional openness, challenging stereotypes and fostering workplace diversity. This paradigm supports dismantling systemic barriers to equality and empowers men to actively participate in creating cultures where everyone feels valued and respected.

Grounded in Positive Psychology, Inclusive Masculinity promotes healthy and equitable expressions of manhood. Scholars like Michael Kimmel and Mark Greene highlight the transformative power of empathy, emotional literacy, and respect. By rejecting harmful stereotypes and embracing emotional vulnerability, men can cultivate self-awareness, strengthen interpersonal relationships, and contribute to environments that prioritize psychological well-being.

This shift does not negate strength but redefines it. True strength lies in collaboration, adaptability, and the courage to challenge societal expectations. By encouraging emotional mastery—understanding and navigating emotions constructively—men can lead with authenticity and inspire cultural shifts within their organizations.

How to Embrace Inclusive Masculinity

1. **Cultivate Emotional Literacy**
   Why it Matters: Emotional literacy—the ability to identify, understand, and express emotions—is foundational for psychological well-being and effective leadership.
   How to Start: Practice labelling your emotions in real-time. For instance, instead of defaulting to "I'm fine," consider whether you feel frustrated, overwhelmed, or hopeful. Journaling can also help you reflect on emotional patterns and triggers.

2. **Develop Empathy Through Active Listening**
   Why it Matters: Empathy bridges divides and fosters

trust, creating environments where people feel understood and valued.

How to Start: Commit to listening without interruption in your conversations. Reflect back on what you hear by paraphrasing, and ask open-ended questions to deepen understanding. For example, "Can you tell me more about how that made you feel?"

3. **Challenge Stereotypes**

   Why it Matters: Breaking free from traditional masculine norms allows men to embrace their full range of strengths and qualities.

   How to Start: When you catch yourself adhering to outdated notions—such as equating vulnerability with weakness—pause and reframe. Ask, "What would strength look like in this situation if I were to show compassion?"

4. **Practice Emotional Mastery**

   Why it Matters: Emotional mastery empowers men to respond thoughtfully rather than react impulsively, fostering constructive outcomes in challenging situations.

   How to Start: Incorporate mindfulness techniques like deep breathing or a brief pause before responding in emotionally charged moments. Acknowledge your feelings without judgment, and choose a response aligned with your values.

5. **Model Inclusivity in Leadership**
Why it Matters: Leaders who exemplify inclusive masculinity inspire others to follow suit, creating a ripple effect throughout the organization.
How to Start: Share personal growth and vulnerability stories in meetings to normalize emotional openness. Actively mentor team members, encouraging their development and recognizing their diverse contributions.

6. **Create Safe Spaces for Dialogue**
Why it Matters: Psychological safety enables individuals to express themselves freely without fear of judgment or reprisal, fostering innovation and collaboration.
How to Start: Set the tone by explicitly inviting input during team discussions. Reinforce that all perspectives are valued and follow up to show how feedback is implemented.

7. **Engage in Continuous Learning**
Why it Matters: Transitioning to inclusive masculinity is a journey, not a destination.
How to Start: Seek out books, podcasts, and workshops

on emotional intelligence, diversity, and leadership. Commit to unlearning biases and replacing them with more inclusive behaviors.

By adopting these practices, men can redefine masculinity as a source of strength, connection, and authenticity. Inclusive masculinity nurtures healthier relationships, strengthens teams, and builds a workplace culture that thrives on trust and mutual respect. These actionable steps empower men to lead intentionally and foster environments where psychological safety and inclusivity are the cornerstones of organizational success.

A Call to Action for Men and Women

Embracing Inclusive Masculinity is not about relinquishing power but reclaiming humanity. It's about breaking free from the constraints of traditional masculinity to lead with empathy and strength, driving personal and organizational growth. Men have a unique opportunity to champion psychological safety, fostering environments where creativity and diversity thrive. By stepping into this evolved role, they can address the *Billion Dollar Blind Spot* at its root—cultural dysfunction.

For women, the role as allies in this transformation is equally vital. Supporting men as they navigate this transition requires understanding and empathy. Women have long been at the forefront of advocating for equality and inclusivity, and now, they can extend their influence by encouraging men to embrace this new paradigm of leadership. It's a partnership that strengthens organizational culture and sets the stage for genuine equality, through the Respect Equality Equation.

Moving forward isn't about rejecting one paradigm for another; it's about embracing the strengths of both. This is the moment to redefine masculinity for the modern workplace—a call to step into a shared vision of progress.

The Strength of Feminine Leadership

We need women who are so strong they can be gentle,
so educated they can be humble, so fierce they can be
compassionate, so passionate they can be rational,
and so disciplined they can be free.
—Kavita Ramdas

One of the epiphanies I had during my recovery from the accident was understanding the strength of femininity, something which I had avoided in my quest to succeed. This is because femininity has often been associated with passivity and dependency, overshadowing the strength, resilience, and leadership capabilities inherent in women. In the evolving corporate landscape, feminine leadership qualities—such as empathy, collaboration, and intuition— are proving to be powerful drivers of success. These traits, often underappreciated in traditional leadership models, reshape how organizations thrive in a dynamic world.

Feminine leadership doesn't replace traditional

masculine strengths but complements them, fostering a balanced approach that embraces decisiveness, collaboration, structure, and adaptability. This synergy unlocks the potential for a thriving, inclusive workplace culture where everyone—regardless of gender—can excel.

And it's not just theory. Research shows that companies with diverse leadership teams are actually more innovative, resilient, and profitable. For example, McKinsey & Company found that gender-diverse executive teams are 21% more likely to outperform their peers financially. Leaders who demonstrate emotional intelligence and foster inclusivity create environments where employees feel valued, engaged, and empowered to contribute their best.

As we explore the strength of feminine leadership, let us recognize the transformative power of balancing these qualities and reimagining leadership as a force for innovation, equity, and collective success.

Traditional Femininity

Scholars such as Judith Butler and Simone de Beauvoir have researched traditional femininity within the framework of societal norms, which has often been associated with traits such as emotional expression, nurturing, empathy, and relational focus. Traditional gender roles have historically depicted femininity as embodying qualities like emotional sensitivity, compassion, and caretaking responsibilities within familial and social contexts. However, societal expectations have also imposed limitations on femininity, reinforcing stereotypes of passivity, emotional dependency, and domesticity.

In contrast to traditional masculinity, which values traits like stoicism, dominance, and aggression, traditional femininity has been characterized by norms of emotional expression, cooperation, and relational sensitivity. Women have often been socialized to prioritize the needs of others, suppress their own desires and ambitions, and conform to restrictive gender roles that confine them to subordinate positions within patriarchal structures.

These concepts of traditional femininity have perpetuated harmful stereotypes and expectations that limit women's autonomy, agency, and opportunities for advancement, thereby impeding their fulfilment of one of our fundamental psychological needs—autonomy, which is crucial for fostering a sense of control, self-determination, and psychological well-being. They have reinforced the notion of women as inherently nurturing and self-sacrificing beings, relegating them to secondary roles in both personal and professional spheres.

Moreover, traditional femininity has usually been linked to ideals of beauty, youthfulness, and physical attractiveness, placing undue pressure on women to conform to narrow standards of appearance and behavior. Traditional media, the fashion industry, and the pervasive influence of social media have amplified this pressure in recent years. Social media, in particular, has created an environment where women face constant scrutiny, often measured against curated and unrealistic portrayals of femininity. However, it also serves as a space where women can challenge these norms, celebrate diverse forms of beauty and leadership, and advocate for autonomy and self-expression. Recognizing and dismantling these constraints is a vital step in empowering women to thrive in all spheres of life.

The Feminist Movement

As society evolves and challenges traditional gender norms, there is a growing recognition of the need to redefine femininity in more empowering and inclusive terms. Embracing a positive and expansive understanding of femininity involves celebrating women's diverse experiences, strengths, and contributions while challenging the stereotypes and expectations that constrain their potential. Doing so entails promoting traits like assertiveness, resilience, and leadership alongside traditionally associated qualities like empathy and compassion.

The discourse around gender has been enriched by

the perspectives of various feminist movements. Alison Jaggar, a prominent feminist philosopher, has delineated different types of feminism, ranging from liberal feminism, which seeks equality within existing societal structures, to radical feminism, which advocates for fundamental social and political change to eliminate the patriarchy system.

These diverse strands of feminism reflect the complexity of gender dynamics and the multiplicity of approaches toward achieving gender equality. While this diversity enriches the movement, it can also send a confusing message about what women want. Some advocate for breaking free from traditional gender roles, while others embrace traditionally feminine qualities as sources of strength. Similarly, debates around career ambitions versus prioritizing family life or seeking equity in male-dominated fields versus creating entirely new leadership paradigms often lead to mixed narratives, resulting in hesitancy on how to move forward even in open-minded workplaces.

The multiplicity of goals and approaches can appear contradictory, making it difficult for organizations and individuals to discern clear pathways for meaningful change. However, this diversity of thought is not actually a weakness; rather, it is a strength that acknowledges the unique needs, aspirations, and experiences of women from all walks of life. Understanding and embracing this multifaceted nature is crucial for crafting inclusive strategies that empower women without imposing a singular definition of success or equality.

It's important to recognize that while feminism has been instrumental in challenging gender-based injustices and advocating for women's rights, the scope of this book goes beyond traditional feminist discourse. Feminism has laid the groundwork for addressing systemic inequalities, but my mission is broader: to champion an ideology rooted in the belief that every individual, regardless of gender identity, possesses inherent dignity and worth—*Respect Equality.*

This approach transcends gender-specific frameworks by fostering a culture of inclusivity that values and empowers men and women alike. By acknowledging the diverse perspectives within feminist discourse, I aim to clarify my commitment to Respect Equality as a guiding principle. This principle seeks to address inequality and inspire a shared vision of mutual respect, collaboration, and empowerment across all aspects of life and leadership.

For male leaders committed to fostering gender equality and respect in their organizations, redefining femininity is about more than challenging entrenched stereotypes. They need to recognize that it is a strategic solution to the billion-dollar problem of disengagement, burnout, and underutilized talent. Creating environments where women can fully express themselves, pursue their goals, and thrive without fear of judgment or discrimination is not merely an ethical imperative, but a business necessity.

Organizations with gender-diverse leadership teams consistently outperform their peers in profitability, innovation, and employee satisfaction. By recognizing and valuing women's unique strengths and perspectives—such as collaborative thinking, emotional intelligence, and a focus on long-term sustainability—male leaders can unlock the untapped potential that drives better decision-making and enhances organizational culture overall.

Embracing an inclusive and empowering vision of femininity is a direct pathway to fostering high-performing workplaces. By leveraging the complementary strengths of all genders, male leaders can create environments where every individual contributes their fullest potential, aligning organizational success with the well-being and empowerment of its people. As we've seen, aspects of traditional masculinity can actively inhibit effective communication among employees, men and women, and prevent a free and effective exchange of ideas. The true strength of an organization lies in its ability to value, respect, and empower every member of its workforce.

In academic research and through the insights of Dr. Pat Heim, it is evident that conflict can often arise between male and female dynamics due to inherent biological, psychological, and cultural differences in their approaches to problem-solving and leadership. Embracing the differences, rather than privileging one approach over another, is key.

Respect Equality recognizes that true progress is achieved when individuals of all genders are empowered to succeed and support each other's success. It fosters a culture of mutual empowerment, where diverse voices and perspectives are celebrated and gender stereotypes are challenged.

So, let's delve deeper into the intricacies of my philosophy on the Respect Equality Model, exploring how it shapes our understanding of gender dynamics and informs our approach to creating inclusive and equitable societies and workplaces. Through reflection, dialogue, and action, we as leaders can strive to pave the way for a future where all individuals, regardless of gender identity, can thrive and contribute to a more just and compassionate world.

Respect Equality:
Unlocking the Power of Collaboration

Respect Equality calls for an intentional shift towards fostering environments that honor the goal-oriented decisiveness often associated with traditional masculinity alongside the process-driven, collaborative strengths frequently linked to femininity. When these complementary approaches are embraced, businesses can unlock the full potential of their teams and create a foundation for innovation, growth, and mutual respect. But it's important to recognize why men often resist changes to this approach.

One day, sitting at a communal table in a local pub, I couldn't help but overhear two men, deeply engrossed in conversation about their day on the job site. Intrigued, I decided to join in, sharing my curiosity about the dynamics of male-dominated industries, particularly regarding the integration of women into these fields.

Mike, a seasoned electrician with years of experience and holding a foreman position, leaned back in his chair, his hands wrapped around his drink. "You know," he began, "this job has been my whole life. My dad was an electrician, and his dad before him. It's more than just a job to us; it feels like it's in our blood."

Nodding in agreement, Tom, a younger plumber, chimed in, "Exactly. It's not just about the skills we've learned; it's about proving ourselves and being reliable and tough. It's a big part of who we are as men."

As I listened, it became evident that their work was more than just a means of livelihood—it was a cornerstone of their identity. Understanding the depth of their connection to their professions, I mentioned how, in environments like theirs, men often anchor their sense of masculinity to their jobs. "Do you think that's why women might resist entering the field?" I asked.

A brief silence followed as Mike and Tom exchanged glances. Mike finally broke it, his tone thoughtful. "Honestly? Maybe. For a lot of guys, this job is where they feel most competent, most themselves. The idea of that changing or being challenged—especially by women, who they're not used to seeing on the job—can feel uncomfortable."

Tom nodded in agreement, adding, "It's not that we doubt women can do the work. It's more about what it means for us if they can. If being a tradesman isn't just a 'guy thing' anymore, what does that say about us? It's like we're having to redefine what it means to be a man in the trades."

Their candid reflections illuminated the deep psychological anchoring of masculinity to their professions—a sentiment echoed in many male-dominated industries. For Mike and Tom, their work wasn't just a career; it was an integral part of their identity, passed down through generations and reinforced by societal expectations.

Broadening the Lens:
Addressing Resistance with Empathy

Their concerns underscored a broader issue: the discomfort that often accompanies cultural and gender shifts within traditionally male-dominated spaces. This resistance isn't inherently about capability; it's about identity and fear of change. For men like Mike and Tom, the entry of women into their fields challenges long-held beliefs about what defines their masculinity.

This moment of vulnerability—where fear and uncertainty met introspection—offered a crucial opportunity. I explained, "Redefining what it means to be a man in your field doesn't take away from your identity; it enhances it. Instead of viewing change as a threat, what if it's an opportunity? Women bring fresh perspectives, new ideas, and complementary skills that can make the work better for everyone."

Mike looked contemplative. "I guess I never thought of it that way. Maybe it's not about losing something; maybe it's about gaining something we didn't even know we needed."

Tom added, "Yeah, like teamwork. If we're all pulling together—men and women—we're stronger. It's not about who's better; it's about being better together."

Actionable Steps for Leaders in Male-Dominated Industries

This interaction highlights the importance of fostering understanding and collaboration between genders in the workplace. Leaders can play a pivotal role in addressing these concerns and creating a culture of respect and inclusion. Here's how:

1. **Facilitate Open Conversations**
   Create spaces where employees can express their fears and uncertainties without judgment. Honest dialogue, like the one with Mike and Tom, can pave the way for understanding and growth.
   Example: Host regular team discussions or workshops to address biases and explore how diversity strengthens the team.

2. **Provide Inclusive Training**
   Offer training that educates employees about the value of diverse teams and equips them with effective collaboration tools.
   Example: Implement programs focusing on emotional intelligence, teamwork, and overcoming unconscious biases.

3. **Celebrate Role Models**
   Highlight men and women in leadership roles who embody collaboration and mutual respect.
   Example: Share stories of successful gender-inclusive teams and the positive outcomes they've achieved.

4. **Frame Change as an Opportunity**
   Help employees see gender diversity as an advantage rather than a threat.
   Example: Share statistics or case studies showing how diversity drives innovation and improves workplace culture.

Redefining Strength Through Collaboration

Mike and Tom's story is a microcosm of the broader journey many male-dominated industries face today. The challenge isn't just about integrating women into these spaces; it's about redefining strength, teamwork, and success through collaboration. By fostering Respect Equality and promoting open dialogue, we can help teams embrace change and evolve into stronger, more innovative units.

When men and women work together, respecting and leveraging their differences, they unlock a synergy that drives progress and enriches the workplace. It isn't about losing something; it's about gaining a richer, more dynamic understanding of what it means to work—and thrive—together.

For many men, their work is more than just a means of livelihood; it represents their competence, reliability, and sense of purpose. This link between profession and identity is subtly reinforced from a young age through societal messages that equate masculinity with providing, protecting, and excelling in traditionally male-dominated fields. Yet, because this connection is rarely discussed or examined, it remains an invisible driver of resistance to change.

Ignoring this dynamic can lead to missed opportunities for meaningful dialogue and growth. When organizations fail to recognize these deeply ingrained identities, efforts to integrate diversity and inclusion initiatives may inadvertently spark defensiveness or resistance. Acknowledging and addressing this connection is crucial for creating strategies that promote inclusivity and honor the identities of those navigating change.

It's important to frame these changes as opportunities to expand and enrich professional identities. This shift allows individuals to view diversity as a complementary force that enhances their roles, rather than a threat to their sense of self.

From a positive psychological perspective, this deep connection to work, while potentially fulfilling, carries risks.

When identity is so tightly interwoven with a profession, setbacks such as job loss, industry changes, or even integrating diversity can trigger feelings of inadequacy, loss, and diminished self-worth. This narrow definition of identity can limit psychological resilience and hinder individuals from exploring other sources of purpose and well-being. To mitigate these risks, fostering a more expansive view of identity—including personal growth, relationships, and values outside of work—becomes essential for sustaining long-term mental health and adaptability.

This anchoring of masculine identity to one's job can be understood through various psychological and sociocultural lenses. From early socialization into gender roles to the validation and belonging derived from working in culturally recognized "masculine" fields, the reasons behind this phenomenon run deep. Historical legacies, economic power, and societal status further cement the connection between work and masculine identity.

Promoting emotional intelligence, embracing diverse role models, fostering community engagement, encouraging personal growth, and prioritizing health and well-being are essential to redefining and broadening masculinity and making room for an expanded definition of femininity as well. By recognizing and celebrating a wider spectrum of attributes and contributions—beyond titles and job roles—we can empower men to find fulfilment and confidence in their masculinity. This approach fosters a healthier, more balanced identity that values individuals for their character, relationships, and resilience, enabling them to thrive both personally and professionally.

Equity initiatives may inadvertently trigger defensiveness or resistance if they fail to recognize how the changes affect personal identity, undermining their effectiveness. By fostering an environment where individuals feel secure in exploring and evolving their identities, we create the psychological safety necessary for genuine engagement with diversity and inclusion efforts. This approach empowers individuals to embrace change, fosters collaboration, and builds the trust required for meaningful cultural transformation, ultimately leading to a more inclusive and equitable society for everyone.

Challenges to Women in the Workplace

Through my conversations with women working in male-dominated industries in both Australia and America, it's become clear that they face multifaceted challenges that extend beyond sexualization. Their experiences often revolve around being undervalued and facing implicit bias that undermines their professional capabilities. For instance, women in American workplaces often recount instances where their ideas are dismissed or attributed to male colleagues, leading to feelings of frustration and invisibility in their roles.

Moreover, women in both countries struggle with systemic barriers to career advancement and equal opportunities. They encounter resistance when seeking leadership positions or opportunities for career progression and feel excluded from informal networks and mentorship opportunities, making it difficult for them to advance in their careers.

Here are four actionable strategies that provide fresh perspectives:

1. **Normalize Gender-Neutral Feedback**: Create systems for performance reviews and feedback that focus on skills, outcomes, and potential rather than gendered perceptions. For instance, avoid using language like "assertive" for men and "aggressive" for women when describing the same behavior. A gender-neutral feedback culture ensures evaluations are fair and constructive.

2. **Reframe Recruitment Messaging**: Review job descriptions and recruitment campaigns to ensure they appeal to diverse candidates. Highlight qualities like collaboration, creativity, and adaptability—traits often undervalued in male-dominated sectors but essential for success—and showcase the organization's commitment to diversity.

3. **Redesign Team-Building Activities**: Shift away from stereotypically male-dominated bonding activities (e.g.,

golf or sports outings) to more inclusive experiences that allow all team members to connect meaningfully. Activities like collaborative workshops, volunteering, or creative challenges foster camaraderie without alienating anyone based on traditional gender norms.

4. **Foster Mixed-Gender Problem-Solving Groups**: Encourage diverse teams to tackle complex challenges together, deliberately mixing perspectives and strengths. For example, creating project groups with balanced gender representation promotes innovative thinking by leveraging both goal-oriented and process-driven approaches, breaking down cultural silos.

Despite the challenges they face, women in male-dominated industries continue to defy stereotypes and make invaluable contributions to their respective fields. Their resilience and innovation challenge outdated norms and add significant value to their industries. Addressing systemic biases and cultural norms through a philosophy of Respect Equality can facilitate the embrace of the unique strengths that women and men each have, bringing all into a more open, effective, and dynamic work environment.

Shifting Perspectives and Overcoming Bias

Gender respect is more than a goal in itself. It is a precondition for meeting the challenge of reducing poverty, promoting sustainable development, and building good governance.
—Kofi Annan.

As many business leaders have learned, making real and substantial changes to a workplace culture involves more than just a set of goals and a slogan. In the realm of industries such as construction, engineering, and technology, perceptions often shape reality in profound ways. For decades, entrenched cultural norms and societal stereotypes have cast a shadow over women's roles and capabilities within these sectors, perpetuating misconceptions and barriers to human respect. This chapter unravels the complex interplay between perception, perception, and reality, shedding light on common misconceptions that hinder progress towards inclusivity and equity.

Perception, the lens through which we interpret the world, plays a pivotal role in shaping our understanding of gender dynamics within male-dominated industries. From ingrained societal beliefs to implicit biases, perceptions significantly influence how men and women are viewed and treated in professional settings, often leading to systemic barriers and discriminatory practices. This contributes to women's marginalization in traditionally male-dominated fields.

Perception is not immutable, however. It is a malleable construct shaped by our experiences, biases, and societal conditioning. By highlighting the discrepancies between the perceptions of women's roles and capabilities and the empirical evidence that challenges these stereotypes, we can explore ways to shift it.

As leaders, we must actively challenge our perceptions, ensuring that facts rather than assumptions or biases inform them. This requires a commitment to self-awareness and a willingness to question our initial judgments and the lens through which we view others. By doing so, we can dismantle the myths and misconceptions that inhibit women's full participation and advancement in male-dominated industries.

Leadership demands the discipline to look at both

sides of the coin. Effective leaders are those who step back and evaluate situations objectively, setting aside personal opinions about the individuals involved. This approach ensures that decisions are fair, equitable, and grounded in reality rather than perception. It also fosters a culture of accountability and inclusivity, where everyone is judged based on their capabilities and contributions rather than preconceived notions.

For example, when faced with a scenario where a woman's ability to lead a project is questioned, leaders must ask themselves:

- Am I basing this judgment on objective evidence or on stereotypes and biases?
- Have I considered her qualifications, track record, and potential contributions?
- How might my personal experiences or opinions about her influence my decision?

They need to look for the spaces between the rungs on that ladder of inference. By asking these questions, leaders can ensure that their perceptions align more closely with reality and create opportunities for women to excel based on merit. This practice empowers individuals and strengthens organizations by tapping into the full spectrum of talent and potential within the workforce.

Ultimately, our perceptions should be dynamic and adaptable, continuously refined by reflection and a commitment to fairness. As leaders, we are responsible for leading by example, questioning our biases and fostering an environment where truth, equity, and progress prevail over unfounded assumptions.

Through a critical examination of perception and reality, this chapter empowers readers with the tools to challenge entrenched norms and foster a culture of inclusivity and equity. Addressing the billion-dollar issue of untapped potential and lost productivity caused by workplace inequality is not just a moral imperative but a business necessity. Misconceptions about women's roles and capabilities in male-dominated industries contribute to systemic barriers that stifle innovation, hinder progress, and perpetuate inequities, costing organizations valuable opportunities for growth and success.

The Value of Shifting Perspectives

Challenging existing norms is not just about equity—it's about securing a competitive advantage. By fostering environments where all individuals can contribute their unique strengths, organizations can enhance their problem-solving capabilities, increase productivity, and improve employee retention.

The journey to inclusivity begins with leaders who are willing to reflect critically on their own perceptions, dismantle biases, and create opportunities for underrepresented talent. This commitment to truth and equity enables organizations to harness the diverse perspectives needed to thrive in an increasingly complex and competitive world. By doing so, we pave the way for a future where workplaces are equitable and engines of innovation and prosperity.

Our ability to confront misconceptions and challenge existing norms is closely linked to our capacity for accountability and self-reflection. The tendency to blame others for our failures can obscure the path to achieving our most ambitious goals and turning challenges into opportunities. Shifting the focus away from blame unveils real opportunities for personal growth and achievement.

In the journey towards gender respect and inclusivity, accountability emerges as a fundamental principle that underpins our ability to effect meaningful change. Drawing on lessons learned from various coaches in both sporting and professional arenas; we uncover a crucial lesson: the significance of accountability and owning our failures. This understanding paves the way to our highest aspirations, transforming obstacles into steppingstones for success.

World-renowned coaches like Vince Lombardi remind us that accountability and resilience are foundational to success. In organizational culture, this principle translates to fostering an environment where individuals are encouraged to take ownership of their actions, learn from setbacks, and continually strive for excellence. Empowering organizational cultures are built on this ethos—valuing effort, fostering growth, and ensuring that challenges are viewed as opportunities for development rather than obstacles to success. By embracing accountability, organizations can inspire a workforce that is motivated, collaborative, and committed to collective achievement.

John Wooden's philosophy underscores another vital leadership lesson: true leaders view failures as stepping-stones for growth. By embracing accountability and fostering a culture of continuous improvement, leaders inspire their teams to adapt, innovate, and thrive in the face of challenges. This resilience transforms setbacks into opportunities and strengthens the foundation for long-term success and collective progress.

Business leaders like Sheryl Sandberg, former COO of Meta, are advocates for owning one's mistakes as a key aspect of leadership. Sandberg famously stated, "Leadership is not bullying, and leadership is not aggression. Leadership is the expectation that you can use your voice for good. That you can make the world a better place." Her words emphasize the importance of humility, authenticity, and accountability in leadership, principles equally applicable in pursuing gender respect.

As we draw inspiration from these renowned coaches and leaders, we recognize that accountability is about taking proactive steps to learn, grow, and effect positive change rather than merely admitting fault. In the context of leadership, this means acknowledging when the current culture of your team or organization is not ideal and accepting the need for change. To shift culture, leaders must first shift perspectives—examining ingrained norms, recognizing biases, and fostering openness to new approaches. By embracing accountability and empowering others, leaders pave the way for dismantling outdated practices, challenging the status quo, and building an inclusive and thriving organizational culture that values growth and innovation.

The concept of "empowered people, empower people" resonates profoundly in this context. In recognizing that human respect is not a zero-sum game but a collective endeavor, we understand that true progress requires the active participation and support of all individuals, regardless of gender. Empowered men who champion gender respect, uplift and advocate for women's rights, create an environment where women are empowered to thrive and contribute fully. Similarly, empowered women who assert their agency and leadership, challenge traditional gender roles while also inspiring and uplifting men to embrace their own vulnerability, authenticity, and potential.

Our tendency to blame others for our failures often

obscures the path to achieving our most ambitious goals and turning challenges into opportunities. When we default to blame, we shift focus away from personal growth and miss the chance to uncover the deeper lessons embedded in our experiences. Perspective plays a critical role here—it allows us to step back, reframe setbacks, and see them not as insurmountable obstacles but as catalysts for growth and improvement.

Learning from various coaches throughout my life, in both sporting and professional contexts, has reinforced the transformative power of accountability. Owning our failures doesn't diminish us; rather, it clears the way to our highest aspirations. By accepting responsibility, we shift our perspective from victimhood to empowerment, recognizing that every misstep holds valuable insights for future success.

This shift in perspective is essential for leading change. Leaders who model accountability inspire their teams to do the same, creating a culture where mistakes are seen as opportunities to innovate and grow. Embracing this mindset fosters resilience and fuels progress, turning setbacks into steppingstones. Ultimately, this approach propels us toward our goals with renewed wisdom and strength and equips us to lead others with authenticity and clarity through the complexities of organizational transformation.

Within male-dominated industries, the pursuit of human respect is fraught with significant challenges. As leaders strive for an empowered organizational culture built on the foundation of respect, they are met with a myriad of challenges that stem from entrenched societal norms and stereotypes, as well as systemic barriers within the industries themselves. In male-dominated industries, some of the top challenges commonly faced by leaders in pursuing gender respect include:

1. **Stereotypical Gender Roles:** Deeply ingrained beliefs about the roles and capabilities of men and women can hinder women's entry and advancement.
2. **Lack of Representation:** A low number of women in leadership positions limits mentorship and role models for aspiring female professionals.
3. **Wage Gap**: Persistent disparities in pay for the same roles and qualifications continue to be a significant issue.
4. **Workplace Culture:** Existing workplace cultures often struggle to support or encourage diversity, inclusivity, or work-life balance, making it challenging for women to thrive.
5. **Access to Opportunities**: Women may face barriers in accessing the same professional development and career advancement opportunities as their male counterparts.

Addressing these challenges requires a concerted effort to change perceptions, policies, and practices to create a more inclusive and equitable working environment. By encouraging a culture where hope is foundational, organizations can empower all members, especially women, to engage fully, pursue growth, and contribute to innovation. This balance between protection and empowerment, coupled with a focus on fostering hope, can transform workplaces into environments where everyone thrives, paving the way for more inclusive and dynamic organizational cultures.

Understanding the Roots of Bias

One afternoon, while sitting down with a group of tradesmen at a job site, I asked a simple question: "Why do you think women hesitate to enter this field?" The men exchanged glances, hesitating, before one of them, let's call him Joe, spoke up.

"It's not that we don't think women can do the work," Joe began, his voice thoughtful. "It's more about... well, what if something happens? These sites aren't exactly safe, and I'd hate to see someone get hurt, especially someone who doesn't know the risks."

I realized he was voicing something deeper—a cultural narrative ingrained in the identity of many men. Historically, men have been cast in the roles of protectors and providers, tasked with shielding those around them from harm. This instinct, while rooted in care, often translates into actions that inadvertently perpetuate gender stereotypes.

Another tradesman chimed in, "Yeah, it's not about doubting their abilities. It's just… if something goes wrong, I'd feel like I failed. Like, it's my job to make sure everyone's okay."

Their words revealed a well-intentioned yet limiting belief system. The instinct to protect women in male-dominated environments often stems from genuine concern, but it unintentionally creates barriers. This narrative, however noble its origins, can send the unintended message that women need special protection, undermining their autonomy and agency.

By the end of our conversation, the men began to reflect on their assumptions. One of them said, "Maybe what we need is to trust that women who choose to be here know the risks, just like we do. Maybe it's not about protecting them but working alongside them."

This moment of clarity was a powerful reminder that beneath resistance often lies a story—a narrative that shapes perception and behavior. Recognizing and rethinking these narratives is the first step in dismantling the barriers that hold women back. It's not about erasing the instinct to care, but about reframing it in a way that empowers everyone to thrive equally. Through honest conversations and storytelling, we can begin to rewrite these cultural scripts, creating spaces where both men and women can step into their full potential, together.

Building the Future:
A Collective Responsibility

As we reflect on these stories and the data that underscores the business case for gender diversity, one truth becomes clear: the time for change is now. These narratives are not isolated anecdotes—they represent a broader, untapped potential waiting to be unleashed across male-dominated industries.

The lessons from this chapter are about acknowledging biases and recognizing our collective responsibility to address them. Empowering women is not just an act of equity but a strategic imperative for organizational growth and innovation. By shifting perceptions, rewriting narratives, and implementing tangible changes, we create workplaces where everyone has the opportunity to thrive and contribute meaningfully.

To lead this change, leaders must prioritize creating cultures where diversity is celebrated, inclusion is non-negotiable, and respect is the foundation. This requires embracing vulnerability, acknowledging existing biases, and fostering an environment where questioning the status quo becomes second nature.

Shifting Perspectives Through Failure

I gasped for air, struggling to the surface of the hydro pool after yet another unsuccessful attempt to stand. Water blurred my vision, and a heavy sense of defeat pressed down on me. In my relentless pursuit to regain my ability to walk, I was faced with a soul-destroying process of falling over time and again. However, the diamond in this darkness was discovering the true power of embracing one's discomfort. This grueling journey of relearning to stand and walk, filled with countless falls, taught me to redefine success and harness failure as a pivotal learning and leadership tool.

Drifting in the pool after an arduous rehabilitation session, I understood that my most formidable obstacle wasn't physical but my mindset. My battle was with my perception of pain, fear and failure. This introspection led to adopting my new guiding principle: 'Fail fast, fail forward.' This mantra became essential for overcoming the immense challenge of walking again, emphasizing the importance of rapidly learning from setbacks to propel myself toward recovery and beyond.

This mindset is desirable and essential in today's corporate landscape, where rapid change and uncertainty are the norms. Leaders must navigate turbulent waters with agility, demonstrating a willingness to learn, adapt, and persevere. The ability to embrace failure as a step toward progress inspires teams, fosters innovation and drives organizations forward. Like students at the University of Hard Knocks, leaders face every difficulty as an exam of their capacity for learning, growth, and the courage to lead through adversity.

Embracing failure is vital; fear can loom large without openness to rapid failure, casting an expansive shadow over our potential. Yet, while painful, failure is not to be feared—it is to be harnessed. In my view, courage is not the absence of fear but a deliberate partnership with it. It's about stepping beyond fear's shadow to master our responses, transforming fear from a limitation into a driver of growth.

This mindset supports the principle of continuous improvement: the concept of striving to be 1% better each day. Small, consistent efforts compound over time, leading to profound personal and professional transformation. By viewing each failure as a steppingstone, we can extract lessons and use them to propel ourselves forward. This incremental growth requires a no-excuse mindset—an unshakable belief in our ability to adapt, learn, and rise stronger after every setback.

Failure, then, becomes not just inevitable but a cherished part of the journey toward success. Each stumble offers a chance to refine our approach, build resilience, and cultivate the habits of continuous self-improvement. In this intimate engagement with failure, we unlock the capacity to transform setbacks into the momentum that drives us toward excellence.

The Failure Analysis Method:
Turning Setbacks into Success

One of the most effective tools I've adopted to shift perspectives is the *Failure Analysis Method*. This structured approach turns failure into a powerful learning experience. It requires us to confront setbacks directly, analyze them with clarity, and extract lessons that fuel growth and resilience. While this process can be uncomfortable, it is indispensable for personal and professional development.

Amy Edmondson's words, *"If you're not failing, you're not journeying into new territory,"* underscore the importance of venturing into the unknown and embracing failure as a necessary part of progress. Below is a step-by-step guide to implementing this method, complete with practical examples to make it actionable:

1. **Identify the Challenge**
   What to do: Clearly define the challenge you faced and the nature of the failure. Write it down.
   Example: A project deadline was missed because of poor time management.

Action: Reflect on what contributed to the missed deadline. Were priorities unclear, procrastination, or lack of delegation?

2. **Analyze Actions**

   What to do: Review your actions or reactions during the challenge. Be objective and remove emotions from the analysis.

   Example: You realize that you spent too much time on low-priority tasks and delayed critical components until it was too late.

   Action: Break down your daily activities and assess where time was misallocated.

3. **Examine Results**

   What to do: Evaluate the outcomes of your actions, focusing on understanding what happened without emotional bias.

   Example: The project wasn't delivered on time, causing delays for the entire team.

   Action: Acknowledge the direct and indirect impacts, such as missed opportunities or strained relationships.

4. **Learn from the Experience**

   What to do: Document key lessons or areas for improvement.

Example: Realize that clearer prioritization and better communication with your team are essential.

Action: Set actionable goals, such as using a task management tool or scheduling regular check-ins with team members.

5. **Address Emotions**

   What to do: Recognize any feelings of shame or frustration tied to the failure. Acknowledge them but don't dwell.

   Example: Feeling embarrassed about letting the team down.

   Action: Reframe your emotions by focusing on the growth potential this experience provides.

6. **Adopt a Growth Mindset**

   What to do: Shift your perspective to view failure as a necessary tool for exploration and improvement.

   Example: Tell yourself, *"This setback has taught me a valuable lesson that will improve my performance in the future."*

   Action: Celebrate the insight gained, even if the experience was challenging.

7. **Commit to Learning**

   What to do: Make a plan to apply the lessons learned and seek opportunities to improve incrementally.

Example: Improve time management by implementing a prioritization framework like Eisenhower's Matrix.

Action: Evaluate your progress regularly to ensure growth becomes a consistent habit.

Success is born from a no-excuse mindset, where struggles are the forge of resilience and determination. To achieve this, we must learn to embrace failure as an intimate partner in the dance toward success. Shifting perspectives and overcoming bias is hard and often involves taking two steps forward and one step back. Through my own journey, I've come to see failure not as a roadblock but as a series of steppingstones, each misstep providing a valuable lesson that draws us closer to our goals. This mindset has transformed how I approach uncertainty and challenges, viewing them not as obstacles but as integral parts of triumph.

Winston S. Churchill's insight, *"Success is stumbling from failure to failure with no loss of enthusiasm,"* captures this concept beautifully. A seamless path to victory does not define leadership and growth, but by the resilience and enthusiasm, we cultivate as we navigate setbacks and challenges. Reframing failure as a growth opportunity, we unlock our potential for continuous improvement on the path to Respect Equality.

Tools to Recognize and Manage Personal and Organizational Biases

Recognizing and managing personal and organizational biases is essential for effective leadership and decision-making. One powerful tool for navigating and understanding biases is the ladder of inference, which helps us understand how ours and others' perceptions and beliefs shape our interpretations of events and interactions. By leveraging the ladder of inference, as leaders we can identify and challenge our biases, fostering more inclusive and equitable organizational cultures.

Firstly, we must cultivate self-awareness to recognize when we need to ascend our the ladder of inference to challenge our mental model. This involves paying attention to our thoughts, emotions, and reactions, questioning the information that is fueling our decisions making. By becoming aware of the cognitive steps involved in forming beliefs and drawing conclusions, we can identify where biases may be influencing our thinking and actions.

To illustrate how we can do this, consider a situation where a manager is evaluating candidates for a promotion within their team. As they review qualifications and performance, the manager notices a tendency to favor individuals who share backgrounds or communication styles similar to their own. This inclination reflects

affinity bias, where the manager unconsciously feels more aligned with candidates who resemble them, leading to assumptions about their compatibility or capability. Such biases influence decision-making at the top rung of the ladder of inference, where subjective preferences shape conclusions, often at the expense of diverse and potentially more qualified candidates. Recognizing and addressing this bias is crucial to ensure equitable and objective decision-making.

The manager engages in reflective practice and mindfulness to cultivate self-awareness and recognize the need to challenge their mental model. They pay attention to their thoughts, emotions, and reactions as they assess each candidate, questioning the information that is driving their decision-making. Through this introspective process, the manager becomes aware of the cognitive steps involved in forming beliefs and drawing conclusions.

To further guide this process, the manager can ask the following three questions after reviewing candidates:

1. **"Am I basing my assessment on objective evidence, or am I being influenced by personal preferences or shared traits?"**
   This question helps the manager distinguish between measurable qualifications and unconscious biases.

2. **"Have I given equal weight to each candidate's contributions and potential, or have I unconsciously favored certain individuals?"**

   This encourages the manager to evaluate all candidates fairly and consider diverse perspectives.

3. **"What additional information or feedback could I seek to ensure my decision aligns with the organization's goals for inclusivity and merit?"**

   This prompts the manager to gather more data and involve others in decision-making, fostering transparency and fairness.

Upon reflection, the manager realizes their preference for candidates with similar backgrounds may stem from unconscious biases, specifically affinity and confirmation biases. Affinity bias occurs when individuals favor those who share similarities with themselves, such as background, communication style, or interests, because these traits evoke a sense of familiarity and comfort. Meanwhile, confirmation bias reinforces this inclination by causing the manager to focus on evidence that supports their preference while overlooking qualifications or strengths that might challenge their assumptions.

By recognizing these biases, the manager acknowledges how their perception of candidates' qualifications and potential for success in the role might be skewed. This realization is critical, as it opens the door for the manager to critically evaluate whether their decision-making process is rooted in objective merit or merely a reflection of their unconscious preferences. By addressing these biases, they can move toward a more equitable and inclusive evaluation process that values diverse skills and perspectives.

With this awareness, the manager decides to climb down the ladder of inference to the bottom rung, where observable data and facts reside. Instead of relying on surface-level impressions or personal preferences, they commit to thoroughly examining a broad range of objective evidence. This includes delving into each candidate's **performance reviews**, which provide documented examples of their strengths, areas for improvement, and growth over time. By comparing these reviews side by side, the manager can identify patterns of consistent performance rather than basing their judgment on isolated instances.

The manager also analyzes **project outcomes**, evaluating tangible contributions each candidate has made to team success. This involves reviewing metrics such as efficiency, innovation, and the quality of deliverables. Are there examples of candidates exceeding expectations or bringing unique solutions to complex challenges? This deeper dive ensures the assessment is grounded in measurable achievements.

Additionally, the manager gathers **feedback from colleagues and stakeholders**, considering how peers, direct reports, and supervisors perceive each candidate. This step is critical to understanding the candidates' ability to collaborate, lead, and influence others—key traits for leadership roles. By synthesizing insights from a variety of sources, the manager ensures their evaluation reflects a comprehensive perspective rather than isolated, biased interpretations.

At this stage, the manager must also reflect on the data they may unconsciously be omitting or undervaluing. Are there accomplishments or skills that challenge their preconceived notions about what makes an ideal candidate? By recognizing how they selectively interpret data, the manager ensures they are fully accounting for each candidate's potential, rather than defaulting to familiar or comfortable choices. This deliberate, inclusive process lays the groundwork for a more equitable and informed decision.

During this process, the manager begins to question how they have been adding meaning to the observed data, recognizing that unconscious biases may have influenced their initial interpretations. For instance, they realize that they previously assigned greater value to qualities like assertiveness or extroversion, aligning with their own communication style, while undervaluing quieter candidates who demonstrate strong analytical and strategic thinking.

To challenge this, the manager consciously broadens their perspective by reframing their criteria for success. Instead of defaulting to traits that mirror their own, they delve into the **specific contributions and contextual significance** of each candidate's strengths. For example, they might consider how a candidate's ability to build consensus has driven team cohesion or how another candidate's deep subject-matter expertise has led to innovative solutions in past projects.

The manager also reflects on how **cultural and systemic factors** may have influenced their interpretations. Are they unconsciously associating leadership potential with traditional, stereotypical traits, such as dominance or charisma, while overlooking other critical qualities like empathy, adaptability, or resilience? This self-awareness prompts them to reassess their understanding of what makes a candidate well-suited for the role, recognizing that diverse leadership styles can equally contribute to organizational success.

Furthermore, the manager takes steps to **seek out evidence that challenges their assumptions actively**. If they had dismissed a candidate for seeming "too inexperienced," they revisit that perception by exploring the candidate's demonstrated ability to take initiative and deliver results under pressure. If they previously viewed another candidate as "too cautious," they consider how that individual's meticulous approach has helped avert risks and ensure project success.

By questioning the meaning, they have ascribed to each candidate's actions and traits, the manager shifts from a subjective to a more balanced and evidence-based evaluation. This process helps mitigate biases and ensures that the final decision is aligned with the organization's broader goals of fostering inclusivity, equity, and diverse leadership styles.

Armed with a heightened sense of self-awareness, the manager is better equipped to make fair and impartial decisions regarding the promotion. Challenging their mental model and questioning their biases ensures that their decision-making process is grounded in objective evidence and fosters inclusivity and equity within the team.

Transforming the Workplace from the Top

We cannot solve our problems with the same thinking we used when we created them.
—Albert Einstein.

In the heart of every challenge lies an opportunity waiting to be seized. This ideology has been the guiding light throughout my journey, from the inception of Empowered Women in Trades—an idea scribbled hastily on a Post-it note—to its evolution into an award-winning business that is reshaping the landscape of Australia's skilled trades industry. At its core, the 30 by 30 mission of Empowered Women in Trades—to increase the representation of women in skilled trades to 30% by 2030—exemplifies the boundless opportunities hidden within even the most daunting challenges.

The story of Empowered Women in Trades is a testament to the transformative power of seeing opportunity where others see obstacles. EWIT's mission uncovers untapped potential in diversifying the workforce in an industry long dominated by tradition and male representation. By bringing women into skilled trades, we address critical labor shortages and challenge stereotypes, fostering innovation and growth within industries that are vital to our economy.

The role of leadership has never been more critical. The rise of AI and automation is not merely altering how we work; it is fundamentally challenging traditional paradigms and reshaping the core of organizational structures. In this transformative landscape, the success of organizations hinges on more than just survival; it demands thriving leadership that ensures human talent remains at the forefront.

Leaders must move beyond viewing their teams as cogs in the machine and instead cultivate an environment where human talent can flourish alongside technological progress. While algorithms and automation excel in efficiency and precision, the uniquely human qualities of creativity, empathy, critical thinking, and adaptability drive true innovation. In this context, thriving as an organization means empowering people to maximize these strengths and harness their full potential.

The responsibility of leaders in this era extends beyond adapting to change; it is about guiding their teams to not only meet challenges head-on but to leverage them as opportunities for growth. This requires fostering a culture where human talent is nurtured and valued—where individuals are not just striving to keep up with technological advancements but are thriving by leading the charge in innovation and collaboration. By prioritizing people's development alongside technology integration, leaders can ensure their organizations remain resilient and competitive while creating meaningful work environments that inspire excellence.

True leadership in this evolving landscape is about recognizing that the future of work is not a competition between human talent and technology; it is a partnership. When leaders embrace this synergy, they unlock the potential for their teams and organizations to survive in the face of change and thrive, setting new benchmarks for success and sustainability.

Becoming Comfortable with Uncertainty

One of the greatest superpowers I've cultivated as a leader is becoming comfortable with uncertainty. Uncertainty is not a hurdle in the ever-changing leadership landscape—it's the proving ground for resilience and innovation. This mindset has enabled me to face ambiguity with confidence, transforming moments of doubt into opportunities for growth. Instead of fearing the unknown, I've embraced it, learning that every decision—whether it results in success or failure—presents a chance to grow, refine my approach, and deepen my understanding of leadership.

In confronting the crippling weight of indecision, I underwent a mindset shift that transformed how I approach challenges. I realized there are no inherently "wrong" decisions, only outcomes that may require adjustment or new strategies. Each outcome offers valuable lessons and insights, reframing setbacks as steppingstones and uncertainty as fertile ground for innovation.

Embracing a No-Excuses Mindset

As the saying goes, a winner is just a loser who kept trying. Resilience is not about avoiding failure but about the willingness to fall down 10 times and get up 11. This no-excuses mindset is critical for leaders navigating today's complexities. It requires relentless commitment to learning, adaptation, and persistence, even when the odds seem stacked against us. This philosophy connects deeply to how we must lead ourselves out of the billion-dollar issue plaguing industries—by fostering cultures where mistakes are embraced as opportunities and perseverance becomes the norm.

Flipping the Tables:
People Over Profit

For far too long, organizations have prioritized profit over people, an approach that is not only unsustainable but counterproductive. Evidence consistently shows that when organizations prioritize people—fostering environments where individuals thrive—profitability follows. Research from the University of Warwick, for example, found that happy employees are 12% more productive, while Gallup data highlights that organizations with engaged employees outperform their peers by 23% in profitability.

Leaders must flip the tables, placing people over profit. This paradigm shift requires creating inclusive cultures where human talent is nurtured, innovation is encouraged, and psychological safety is prioritized. By doing so, organizations not only unlock the full potential of their teams but also achieve stronger financial performance and long-term sustainability.

A Practical Framework for Resilient Leadership

1. **Own Your Decisions**: When faced with uncertainty, consider the best- and worst-case scenarios. Count down from five to one, make the decision, and commit

to it with resolve. Doubt and second-guessing only stall progress.

2. **Reframe Failures**: View mistakes as lessons, not setbacks. Every misstep provides insight into how to move forward more effectively. As leaders, we must model this mindset for our teams, demonstrating that growth often stems from discomfort.

3. **Prioritize People**: Build cultures where employees feel valued and empowered. Invest in their growth, foster open communication, and create environments where they can thrive. This focus not only enhances individual well-being but also drives organizational success.

4. **Lead with Resilience**: Embrace a no-excuses mindset. Resilience is built through persistence, adaptability, and the willingness to tackle challenges head-on. As leaders, our ability to rise from setbacks inspires others to do the same.

Leadership in this era of rapid change demands courage, adaptability, and an unwavering commitment to growth. By becoming comfortable with uncertainty, embracing resilience, and flipping the focus from profit to people, we not only navigate today's challenges but transform them into opportunities. This is how we lead ourselves—and our organizations—out of the billion-dollar issue and toward a future defined by thriving, not just surviving.

Embracing Fear to Lead Change:
Transforming Leadership in Male-Dominated Industries

The perception of the "fearless leader" in male-dominated industries is a myth that can be more harmful than inspiring. Fear is a universal experience, even among the most accomplished leaders. What sets transformative leaders apart is their ability to navigate fear, using it as a tool to fuel courage and drive change.

Instead of avoiding fear, leaders can and should harness it to challenge norms and champion diversity. For instance, confronting biases or outdated practices requires acknowledging discomfort and moving through it to build equitable workplaces. This isn't just a moral imperative—it's a financial one. Research consistently shows that diverse and inclusive organizations perform better, with higher innovation rates and increased profitability.

The Need for Stillness in a World of Stimulation

We are bombarded by constant stimulation in today's fast-paced, technology-driven landscape. Notifications, emails, and endless demands keep our minds perpetually busy, leaving little room for introspection or creativity. Yet it is in stillness that leaders find clarity and the strength to confront their fears.

Practicing mindfulness—a concept often dismissed as "new age" but actually grounded in science—is no longer optional for effective leadership. Mindfulness helps leaders regulate emotions, focus attention, and make better decisions. By proactively creating moments of stillness, leaders cultivate the resilience to face fear and uncertainty head-on, transforming challenges into opportunities.

To address the *Billion Dollar Blind Spot*, leaders must shift from prioritizing profits to focusing on people. This isn't a call to abandon financial goals; it's a recognition that investing in human talent leads to better business outcomes. Studies show that organizations prioritizing employee well-being see increased productivity, lower turnover, and higher profits.

This shift requires a no-excuses mindset—leaders must fall down ten times and get up eleven. Resilience isn't optional; it's a requirement. A winner, as they say, is simply a loser who kept trying. By embracing failure as part of the growth process, leaders demonstrate that setbacks are steppingstones to success, inspiring their teams to persevere.

Practical Strategies for Leading Through Fear

To lead effectively through fear and uncertainty, consider these actionable steps:

1. **Create Stillness:** Dedicate time each day for mindfulness practices, such as deep breathing or meditation, to clear your mind and sharpen your focus.
2. **Reframe Challenges:** View failures as opportunities for learning. Each misstep offers insights that can propel your growth.
3. **Commit to People Over Profit:** Invest in initiatives that enhance employee well-being and foster inclusion. Empowered teams drive better financial outcomes.
4. **Model Resilience:** Share your own experiences of overcoming fear and failure, showing your team that vulnerability and perseverance are strengths.

Reflecting on my journey—relearning to walk and founding Empowered Women in Trades—I've learned that fear is not the enemy. It's a powerful motivator that, when embraced, leads to profound growth. By walking alongside fear, I've challenged societal norms, advanced gender respect, and redefined leadership in male-dominated spaces.

For leaders, the path forward is clear: embrace fear as an ally. Use it to spark innovation, drive inclusion, and transform your organization. Together, we can pioneer a future where leaders rise above fear, prioritize people, and dismantle the billion-dollar barriers holding workplaces back.

Your journey begins now. Embrace fear, act with courage, and lead your organization toward a thriving, inclusive future.

Transforming Diversity Strategies:
Building True Inclusivity Through Mentorship, Support, and Feedback

Traditional diversity strategies often prioritized numbers over nuance, focusing on increasing representation without tackling the deep-rooted systemic barriers that prevent true inclusivity. While representation is a critical first step, it's not a silver bullet. True inclusion requires organizations to address the culture, structural and psychological inequality and hinder collaboration, innovation and growth. Organizations must move beyond checkbox diversity and commit to a holistic transformation to create workplaces where everyone can truly thrive. This involves fostering environments where individuals (including men) feel values, respected and empowered to contribute their full potential. Central to this effort are some key pillars which we will explore below.

The Importance of Female Mentors for Men

Female mentors can bring transformative perspectives to male colleagues, broadening their understanding of diverse leadership approaches and challenging ingrained biases. For men, having a female mentor offers insights into women's experiences in male-dominated fields, fostering empathy and collaboration.

Practical Example: A male executive in construction may work with a female mentor from engineering, gaining a fresh perspective on navigating challenges she experiences so he can understand how to become an ally and truly lead inclusively. This mentorship bridges gaps in understanding and creates allies for systemic change.

Succession Planning and Support

Pushing women into roles without adequate preparation and support sets them up for failure, perpetuating harmful stereotypes about gender and capability. True diversity requires intentional succession planning and resources to help women succeed in leadership roles.

Practical Steps to Support Women in male-dominated industries to thrive:

1. **Individual Development Plans:** Pair emerging female leaders with mentors and provide tailored training to address specific skill gaps.

2. **Onboarding Programs:** Design comprehensive onboarding processes that equip women in leadership roles with the tools and support networks they need to excel.

3. **Checkpoints for Success:** Establish regular review points to assess progress, identify challenges, and adjust strategies to ensure long-term success.

Leveraging Male Wisdom to Empower Women

Men have historically had greater access to leadership opportunities, giving them a wealth of knowledge about navigating the war room of the board room. Sharing this wisdom with women can be a powerful way to empower the next generation of leaders. This isn't about diminishing men's achievements but using their experience to accelerate gender equity.

Practical Example: A senior male leader in a technology firm creates a "knowledge transfer program" to share strategies, lessons, and best practices with female employees aspiring to leadership.

Moving Beyond Tokenism

It's not enough to simply place women in visible positions; organizations must ensure these roles are meaningful and impactful. Representation without substance risks undermining the progress toward true diversity.

Practical Step: Pair diversity metrics with impact metrics. Measure the number of women in leadership and their influence on decision-making, team outcomes, and organizational culture.

Strategies for Building Effective Feedback Loops

1. **Create Safe Spaces**

   Positive psychology teaches us that belonging and security are foundational for personal and professional growth. To foster open communication:

   Anonymous Channels: Implement systems like anonymous surveys or digital feedback platforms to reduce fear of repercussions.

   Moderated Discussions: Host facilitated forums where employees can discuss sensitive issues, knowing their voices will be heard without judgment.

   Example: A construction firm created a "Voice of the Team" initiative, enabling anonymous submission of challenges. One employee suggested updating safety protocols, which led to an actionable improvement, building trust across the team.

2. Normalize Constructive Feedback

Constructive feedback thrives in a culture that views mistakes as learning opportunities. Training managers in delivering feedback with empathy and clarity ensures a strengths-based approach:

Actionable and Bias-Free: Focus on specific behaviors and outcomes rather than vague critiques. For instance, replace "Your presentation was weak" with "Focusing more on data visuals can strengthen your presentations."

Recognizing Strengths First: Begin feedback conversations with a recognition of the employee's unique strengths and contributions, tying areas for growth back to their potential.

Example: A manager in a tech company began team meetings with a "win of the week," highlighting individual achievements before discussing improvement opportunities. This shifted the team's mindset from fear of criticism to a collaborative growth-oriented culture.

3. Close the Loop

Feedback without follow-through erodes trust.

Demonstrating that employee insights lead to tangible actions solidifies the value of their input:

Implement and Communicate Changes: After gathering feedback, act on it promptly and communicate the changes to employees. Use meetings, newsletters, or internal platforms to highlight what was heard and how it's being addressed.

Feedback on Feedback: Regularly solicit input on the feedback process itself. Is it effective? Do employees feel heard?

Example: A manufacturing company that gathered quarterly feedback discovered that inconsistent shift schedules were harming work-life balance. After making adjustments, they shared this success story with employees, reinforcing the value of their input and building a sense of shared achievement.

Cultivating Psychological Safety Through Positive Psychology

To deepen the impact of feedback loops, leaders must embed psychological safety into the organizational fabric:

- **Model Vulnerability:** Leaders who admit their own mistakes create a ripple effect of openness. A senior manager who shared a personal learning moment during a leadership retreat set a tone of humility and authenticity for their team.

- **Celebrate Effort and Growth:** Recognize not just outcomes but also employees' effort and learning processes. This reinforces the idea that growth is a journey, not a destination.
- **Active Listening as a Habit:** Encourage leaders to practice active listening during feedback sessions. Techniques such as summarizing key points, avoiding interruptions, and asking open-ended questions signal genuine engagement.

As a leader, ensure you are utilizing feedback loops as a powerful tool for successful organizational change. It gives you opportunities to amplify the voices of those who may have been unheard, allowing you to empower diversity and inclusion truly. By integrating the principles of positive psychology, you can create environments where employees feel valued, empowered, and motivated to contribute their best.

Ask yourself:

- Are my feedback systems inclusive and empowering?
- Do they foster growth or perpetuate fear?
- How can I, as a leader, model psychological safety and strengths-based feedback?

When feedback becomes a tool for connection, growth, and mutual respect, it transforms workplaces into thriving ecosystems of innovation and inclusion. Let's redefine feedback as a powerful driver of transformation that allows the organization to continuous improve, grow and thrive.

A Culture of Learning and Continuous Improvement:
A Positive Psychology Approach

Creating a culture of learning and continuous improvement allows organizations to evolve alongside the diverse needs of their workforce, fostering a thriving and inclusive environment. Diversity and inclusion are not endpoints to be reached; they are dynamic, ongoing commitments that require organizations to continually learn, adapt, and grow. Incorporating continuous learning through a positive psychology lens ensures that diversity initiatives are not seen as obligations but as opportunities to enhance individual and organizational well-being.

Practical Strategies for Building a Learning Culture

1. Invest in Leadership Training: Building Inclusive Competence

Leaders set the tone for the entire organization and equipping them with the skills to lead inclusively is critical. Effective leadership training should address:

- **Emotional Intelligence (EQ):** Leaders with high EQ are better equipped to navigate diverse perspectives with empathy and understanding. For example, a retail company implemented EQ workshops where leaders learned to listen actively and respond thoughtfully to emotional cues, leading to stronger team cohesion.

- **Unconscious Bias Awareness:** Training that helps leaders identify and mitigate their biases fosters fair decision-making. Use interactive exercises like anonymized decision-making simulations to make the learning tangible.

- **Inclusive Leadership Skills:** Equip leaders to advocate for underrepresented groups and foster team belonging. For instance, a construction firm trained supervisors to facilitate inclusive team meetings, ensuring every voice was heard.

Positive Psychology Connection: Training focused on equity and inclusivity aligns with positive psychology's emphasis on fostering strengths and enhancing relationships. When leaders learn to recognize and amplify the unique strengths of their teams, they create environments where everyone can thrive.

2. **Celebrate Milestones: Sustaining Momentum with Positive Emotions**
   Celebrating achievements is a powerful way to sustain motivation and reinforce the organization's commitment to diversity. Recognition fosters positive emotions, which in turn fuel resilience and engagement:

   - **Highlight Individual Contributions:** Share success stories of individuals who've driven diversity initiatives. For example, a logistics company created an "Inclusion Champion" award to honor employees who contributed significantly to fostering inclusivity.
   - **Acknowledge Team Successes:** Celebrate team milestones, such as reaching diversity hiring goals or launching a new mentorship program. Public recognition through newsletters, meetings, or social media channels reinforces the organization's priorities.
   - **Annual Reflections:** Use events like a Diversity Week or annual company gathering to reflect on progress

and set new goals, creating a rhythm of continuous improvement.

Positive Psychology Connection: Celebration aligns with the PERMA framework's Positive Emotions and Accomplishment pillars. Recognizing milestones reinforces a sense of pride and collective achievement, strengthening both individual and organizational well-being.

Cultivating a Growth-Oriented Mindset

To embed a culture of learning, organizations must shift from a static mindset to one that embraces growth and adaptation. Positive psychology offers tools to nurture this mindset:

- **Normalize Mistakes:** Frame mistakes as opportunities to learn and grow. For example, a software company created "Lessons Learned" sessions where teams could openly discuss challenges without fear of blame.
- **Encourage Feedback as a Learning Tool:** Create a two-way feedback culture where leaders and employees learn from each other. For instance, reverse mentoring programs that allow junior employees to share insights with senior leaders should be introduced.
- **Celebrate Effort Over Perfection:** Recognize the hard

work and progress involved in pursuing diversity initiatives, even if all goals aren't met immediately.

To build a learning and continuous improvement culture, leaders must champion the process as an ongoing journey rather than a box to check. Ask yourself:

- Am I equipping my team with the tools to grow and learn?
- How do I celebrate and sustain momentum for our diversity initiatives?
- Are we creating safe spaces where mistakes are embraced as learning opportunities?

By adopting a mindset of continuous learning and growth, leaders enhance diversity and inclusion and lay the foundation for lasting organizational resilience and success. Together, we can transform learning into a shared journey of empowerment, innovation, and progress one that benefits every individual and the collective whole.

Implementing Gender Diversity:
Practical Strategies for Inclusion, Belonging, and Innovation

The journey to achieving genuine gender diversity in male-dominated industries demands more than traditional approaches it calls for bold thinking, innovative strategies, and a commitment to building a culture of inclusivity. It's not just about increasing representation; it's about dismantling systemic barriers, unlocking potential, and creating workplaces where everyone can thrive. By embracing creativity, empathy, and strategic inclusivity, organizations can transform diversity from a challenge into a powerful driver of growth and innovation.

As leaders, our role is to create an environment where innovation flourishes, employees feel empowered to contribute their unique talents, and everyone experiences a genuine sense of belonging. Through this commitment to rethinking and evolving, we can turn obstacles into opportunities for meaningful progress.

The following strategies showcase this mindset's potential, offering practical and innovative ways to empower employees, celebrate diversity, and cultivate a workplace culture that inspires belonging. These approaches are not just tools but pathways to transformation, ensuring that every team member feels valued, supported, and positioned to succeed.

Rethink Transferable Skills:
Recognizing Talent Beyond Traditional Criteria

Consider the example of a woman re-entering the workforce after 10 years as a stay-at-home mother. Instead of viewing her absence from formal employment as a gap, recognize the incredible skills she honed during that time:

- **Time Management:** Coordinating schedules, managing household activities, and meeting multiple deadlines.
- **Multitasking:** Balancing competing priorities under pressure.
- **Conflict Resolution:** Mediating disputes and fostering harmonious relationships within the family.
- **Budget Management:** Overseeing financial planning and resource allocation.

Actionable Step: Integrate transferable skills into recruitment criteria. When reviewing applications, look beyond titles and roles to experiences demonstrating leadership, adaptability, and problem-solving.

Reimagine Company Events

Company events often skew towards specific preferences, unintentionally excluding segments of the workforce.

For example, hosting all events at pubs or sports venues may alienate those who prefer quieter or more family-friendly activities.

Actionable Step: Survey employees to understand their preferences and organize a diverse array of events. Examples include:

- Family-inclusive picnics.
- Skill-building workshops.
- Volunteer days for community service.

Outcome: This approach demonstrates respect for different lifestyles and interests, fostering a culture of inclusion and belonging.

Designing True Succession Planning and Mentorship

As discussed earlier women are often promoted without adequate preparation or support, creating a cycle of perceived failure that reinforces harmful stereotypes. A strategic approach to succession planning and mentorship ensures long-term success.

Practical Steps:

- **Structured Mentorship Programs:** Pair aspiring female leaders with experienced mentors who can provide guidance, share insights, and model effective leadership.
- **Progressive Role Development:** Transition women into leadership roles gradually, ensuring they build the skills and confidence needed for long-term success.
- **Feedback and Support:** Implement ongoing performance reviews with actionable development plans tailored to each leader's needs.

Example: A tech firm implements a six-month leadership incubation program for women, combining mentorship, leadership training, and stretch assignments.

Passing Down Male Wisdom to Empower Women

Men in leadership positions have accumulated significant experience navigating organizational dynamics. Sharing this knowledge empowers women and fosters collaboration.

Actionable Step: Host "Leadership Knowledge Exchange" sessions where male leaders share lessons learned and practical insights. Ensure sessions are collaborative, with opportunities for dialogue and mutual learning.

Fostering a Sense of Belonging

Belonging is the foundation of employee engagement and retention. Inclusive initiatives go beyond diversity metrics to create a workplace where everyone feels valued and integral to the team's success.

Practical Strategies to Inspire Belonging:

- **Celebrate Individual Contributions:** Recognize achievements across all levels through shout-outs, newsletters, or awards.
- **Create Affinity Groups:** Support employee resource groups where individuals with shared experiences can connect and advocate for positive change.
- **Encourage Open Dialogue:** Organize regular town halls where employees can voice ideas and concerns, fostering a sense of agency and connection.

The cost of clinging to outdated approaches in diversity and inclusion is staggering both financially and culturally. Organizations with inclusive cultures consistently outperform their peers, driving greater profitability, innovation, and employee satisfaction. Conversely, disengagement, turnover, and missed opportunities contribute to the *Billion Dollar Blind Spot*, holding businesses back from their true potential.

The path forward demands creativity, empathy, and a willingness to push boundaries. Step into the discomfort of not knowing and use it as fuel for discovery. Lead by example, inspiring your team to collaborate, innovate, and shape a workplace where everyone can thrive. The future of your organization—and the incredible potential of your people—depends on it. Now is the time to act.

Evolving Leadership Styles:
Moving from Control to Empowerment

As organizations navigate the complexities of modern challenges, leadership styles must evolve to address both the human and financial costs of outdated practices. The transformation from traditional, top-down leadership to inclusive, empowering approaches is essential to resolving the *Billion Dollar Blind Spot*. Leaders must embrace practices that empower their teams, foster trust, and enhance psychological safety while addressing common pitfalls like micromanagement and ineffective delegation.

Are You a Micromanager?

Micromanagement is often a silent but powerful contributor to workplace inefficiencies, disengagement, and turnover, exacerbating the *Billion Dollar Blind Spot*. Yet, many leaders who micromanage are unaware of their tendencies. Rooted in fear of failure, a desire for control, or an overly high standard of perfection, micromanagement can undermine trust and stifle team growth. Recognizing this behavior is the first step toward cultivating an empowered and productive team.

Why Do We Micromanage? At its core, micromanagement often stems from a fear of losing control, a lack of trust in others, or an internal belief that our way is the only right way. These tendencies can be exacerbated by:

- **Perfectionism:** The belief that the work must meet an unreasonably high standard only achievable by direct intervention.
- **Insecurity:** Fear of being held accountable for mistakes or feeling inadequate as a leader.
- **Habitual Control:** A mindset that leadership equals oversight of every detail.
- **Lack of Awareness:** A genuine unawareness of how one's actions impact the team's morale and autonomy.

Understanding the psychology behind micromanagement can help leaders reframe their approach to delegation and leadership. Positive psychology reminds us that creating environments where individuals feel trusted, competent, and valued is essential for fostering growth and engagement.

Self-Reflection Checklist: Are You Micromanaging?
Use the following checklist to assess your tendencies. Answering "yes" to any of these questions might indicate micromanagement tendencies:

1. Do you frequently override or redo your team's work, even if it meets the requirements?
2. Do you require constant updates, often unnecessarily?
3. Do you struggle to delegate without giving detailed, step-by-step instructions?
4. Do your team members hesitate to make decisions independently and wait for your approval instead?
5. Do you feel anxious or out of control when you're not involved in every detail of a project?

If you see yourself in any of these behaviors, it's not a sign of failure—it's an opportunity to grow and enhance your leadership style. Recognizing these tendencies is the first step toward creating a more empowering work environment.

Actionable Steps to Transition from Micromanagement to Empowered Leadership

1. **Reflect and Accept:** Begin by acknowledging the impact of your behavior. Reflect on specific instances where you've micromanaged and consider the outcomes. Were they worth the energy? Did they build trust, or did they inadvertently discourage your team? Recognizing the "why" behind your actions can help shift your mindset.

2. **Empower Through Delegation:**
   - Assign tasks by defining clear outcomes and expectations, but leave the "how" up to your team members.
   - Focus on the big picture and resist the urge to dictate minor details.
   - Trust that your team has the capability to innovate and deliver results. This fosters creativity and accountability.

3. **Reframe Control as Support:**
   - Instead of asking, "How can I ensure this is done my way?" ask, "How can I support my team in achieving the best outcome?"
   - Position yourself as a coach, not a taskmaster. Offer guidance when needed but step back to let others take ownership.

4. **Develop Emotional Resilience:**
   - Use positive psychology tools, such as gratitude and mindfulness, to manage feelings of anxiety about relinquishing control.
   - Practice self-awareness by journaling or reflecting daily on your interactions with your team.

5. **Foster Psychological Safety:**
   - Encourage open communication where team members feel safe discussing their challenges without fear of criticism or micromanagement.
   - Celebrate mistakes as learning opportunities, reinforcing that errors are part of growth.

6. **Create a Feedback Loop:**
   - Regularly ask your team for feedback on your leadership style. Questions like "Do you feel empowered in your role?" or "Is there anything I can do differently to support you better?" can reveal blind spots.
   - Act on this feedback to continuously improve your approach.

7. **Recognize and Celebrate Competence:**
   - Focus on your team's strengths and successes. Recognizing their achievements helps build their confidence and reinforces your trust in their abilities.

- Highlight and celebrate progress, even on small wins, to shift your mindset from oversight to celebration.

Example of Empowered Leadership in Action: Imagine leading a project where you typically micromanage every detail. Instead, you define clear objectives, communicate the desired outcome, and encourage the team to take ownership. By the project's end, a team member innovates a solution you hadn't considered. Not only does this save resources, but it also boosts their confidence and sets a precedent for future collaboration. You've transitioned from a control-focused leader to one who inspires innovation and growth.

Micromanagement isn't an endpoint it's a starting line for transformation. By recognizing these tendencies and committing to change, you're improving your leadership and creating an environment where your team can thrive. Embrace vulnerability, lean into trust, and let go of the need for control. Leadership isn't about doing everything yourself but empowering others to succeed.

Active Listening:
The Leadership Superpower for Innovation and Inclusion

Active listening a leadership superpower. In addressing the challenges we face as leaders, active listening is a transformational tool that enables us to uncover hidden challenges we are unaware of, explore untapped opportunities, and build trust within our teams. It is the bridge between what we think we know and what we must learn to create inclusive, dynamic, and innovative environments.

Why Active Listening Matters in This Journey

Too often, leaders listen to respond rather than to truly understand. This reactive approach can perpetuate blind spots, misunderstandings, and missed opportunities. Active listening requires leaders to be present, empathetic, and curious qualities that are essential for addressing complex issues like gender diversity and fostering inclusion.

In male-dominated industries, where systemic barriers often go unspoken, active listening is the key to discovering what we don't know. It empowers leaders to tap into the lived experiences of their teams, creating a culture of psychological safety where individuals feel valued and heard. By listening actively, leaders build trust and invite collaboration and co-design, transforming challenges into opportunities.

The Science Behind Active Listening and Positive Psychology

Active listening aligns with principles of positive psychology by fostering genuine connection and engagement. When leaders actively listen, they convey respect and empathy, which are foundational to psychological safety. This approach also nurtures relatedness, one of the core psychological needs identified in Self-Determination Theory, driving motivation and well-being.

Moreover, active listening helps leaders uncover strengths within their teams, enabling them to harness diverse perspectives for creative problem-solving. By giving space for open dialogue, leaders can foster a sense of belonging and co-create innovative strategies to address organizational challenges.

Practical Exercises to Build Active Listening Habits

Building the habit of active listening requires intention and practice. Here are two simple yet powerful exercises to enhance your skills:

1. **The Notebook Method**
   - Keep a notebook during conversations and mark

a line every time you catch yourself wanting to interrupt, judge, or prepare a response before the speaker has finished.

- At the end of the day, review the marks and reflect on patterns. Are there particular situations or individuals where your active listening lapses? Use these insights to set goals for improvement.

2. **The Rubber Band Trick**
   - Wear a rubber band on your wrist and gently flick it whenever you notice your focus drifting or your urge to interrupt.
   - This tactile reminder creates awareness and helps rewire your brain to prioritize listening overreacting.

Active Listening Checklist:
Transforming Conversations into Solutions

1. **Be Present**
   - Focus entirely on the speaker, maintaining eye contact and setting aside distractions like phones or emails.
   - Practice mindfulness to stay in the moment and engage fully with what is being said.

2. **Suspend Judgment**
   - Avoid forming opinions or preparing responses while

the speaker is talking. This openness allows for deeper understanding and mutual respect.

3. **Paraphrase and Clarify**
   • Reflect back what you've heard to confirm understanding. Phrases like, "What I'm hearing is…" or "Can you elaborate on that?" demonstrate engagement and encourage deeper dialogue.

4. **Ask Thoughtful Questions**
   • Use open-ended questions to explore perspectives further. For example, "What challenges do you see in implementing this idea?" or "How can we support this more effectively?"

5. **Acknowledge and Validate**
   • Show appreciation for the speaker's input. Simple affirmations like, "Thank you for sharing that perspective" or "I hadn't considered it that way" reinforce the value of their contribution.

Why This Matters for Innovation and Inclusion

Active listening is the gateway to uncovering the unknown. It allows leaders to:

- **Identify Root Causes:** By understanding the lived experiences of team members, leaders can pinpoint systemic barriers that need to be addressed.
- **Co-Create Solutions:** Active listening fosters collaboration, where diverse perspectives merge to create innovative approaches to challenges.
- **Build Inclusive Cultures:** When individuals feel heard and valued, they are more likely to contribute authentically, enhancing engagement and belonging.

As leaders, we often feel the pressure to have all the answers, but true leadership lies in the willingness to listen and learn. Active listening is not passive; it is a courageous commitment to understanding, growing, and innovating alongside your team.

Embrace active listening as a tool to transform challenges into opportunities. Lean into the discomfort of not knowing, and use it as an invitation to explore what is possible. By listening deeply, you can uncover insights that address the *Billion Dollar Blind Spot* and create a culture of respect, empowerment, and limitless potential.

The Road Ahead:
Stepping Boldly Into the Future of Leadership

Today, leadership is a journey defined not by comfort but by courage. The challenges we face from fostering diversity and inclusion to embracing innovation and navigating rapid change are not barriers but invitations to grow. Our challenges call us to reimagine leadership as an act of curiosity, creativity, and unrelenting determination to embrace a philosophy of true Respect Equality.

The *Billion Dollar Blind Spot*—the disengagement, inefficiency, and exclusion that afflicts workers—stands as a stark reminder of what is at stake. Yet, within this challenge lies an unparalleled opportunity. Research consistently demonstrates that organizations prioritizing inclusion, psychological safety, and innovation achieve higher profitability, increased employee satisfaction, and enhanced productivity. The evidence is clear: the way forward demands bold action.

As leaders, the first step is to embrace the "incompetence curve," recognizing that growth often begins where our confidence ends. Whether facing fears of failure or navigating uncharted territory, our ability to push through discomfort is the catalyst for meaningful change. When we view uncertainty not as a weakness but as fertile ground for innovation, we unlock our full potential—and that of our teams.

How to Rise to the Challenge

1. **Acknowledge the Opportunity Within the Challenge**
   Reframe every obstacle as an opportunity to grow, innovate, and lead differently. Ask yourself: What could we achieve if we approached this challenge with creativity and courage?

2. **Embrace a People-First Paradigm**
   Shift your focus from profits to people, understanding that when employees thrive, so do organizations. Create environments where every individual feels valued, heard, and empowered to contribute their best.

3. **Commit to Continuous Growth**
   The journey of leadership is never complete. Cultivate a culture of learning within your organization by embracing feedback, celebrating effort, and normalizing mistakes as part of growth.

4. **Be Vulnerable and Take Risks**
   True leadership requires stepping into the unknown, admitting when you don't have all the answers, and co-designing solutions with your teams. By doing so, you model the courage and adaptability needed to address complex challenges.

The Future is Yours to Shape

The issues we face as leaders—whether systemic inequality, resistance to change, or the evolving demands of the workplace—are complex, but they are not insurmountable. They are not obstacles to resent but privileges to embrace. They signify the trust others place in us, our opportunities to make a difference, and our potential to grow and lead. Viewing pressure through this lens transforms it from a source of stress to a catalyst for strength, resilience, and achievement.

This mindset shift is essential for navigating the challenges of leadership and personal growth. It allows us to see discomfort not as an enemy but as an ally—a signal that we are on the edge of transformation. Just as my countless falls in the hydro pool were steps toward reclaiming my ability to walk, the pressures we face in leadership are steppingstones to becoming the leaders we aspire to be. Embracing this privilege requires courage, self-compassion, and the willingness to persist despite setbacks. In doing so, we rise above our challenges and inspire those around us to do the same.

Transforming Yourself: Harnessing Character Strengths

*Character is the real foundation
of all worthwhile success*
—John Hays

Change often needs to come from the top – but sometimes, even most of the time, you may not be the one in charge. But that doesn't mean you can't shift a workplace culture or your experience within an organization. It starts with yourself—your own unique strengths and skills.

On the first day of every new year, I make a point of revisiting my character strengths profile. It's become a ritual of reflection and renewal that sets the tone for the year ahead. This year was no different, and as I pored over my results, my top strengths—humor, love of learning, gratitude, fairness, and hope—a roadmap for navigating the complexities of life and leadership started to unfold.

Humor, my top strength, shows me that I have the

responsibility to ensure I bring the power of lightness and connection daily to even the most serious situations. Whether it's using a well-timed quip to ease tension in a high-stakes meeting or simply sharing a laugh with my team, humor creates a bond that transcends workplace roles and reminds us of our shared humanity. Love of learning fuels my insatiable curiosity, pushing me to constantly seek new knowledge and ways to grow—traits that have been critical in my journey as both a leader and a perpetual student of life. Gratitude grounds me, fairness guides my decisions, and hope propels me forward, even when the path is unclear.

As I reflect on these strengths, I'm struck by how they shape my personal approach to challenges and my vision for fostering dynamic, high-performing teams. In leadership, I've learned that understanding our character strengths— and those of our team members—is a game-changer. It's the difference between a group of individuals working in silos and a cohesive team thriving through collaboration, innovation, and trust. Whether you're a leader or a member of the team, understanding what you bring to the table, and what everyone else does as well, is essential for a high-functioning work environment.

The concept of character strengths isn't new. Its roots lie in the field of positive psychology, which we've discussed earlier. In addition to developing PERMA, Seligman and Peterson's work led to the VIA (Values in Action) Classification of Strengths and Virtues, which identifies 24 universal character strengths grouped under six broad virtues: wisdom, courage, humanity, justice, temperance, and transcendence. These strengths aren't just traits; they're a lens through which we can view human potential and flourishing.

Integrating these strengths into leadership and team dynamics isn't theoretical—it's deeply practical. Take my strength in fairness, for example. It influences how I approach decision-making, ensuring that every voice is heard and considered, whether we're discussing a new business strategy or resolving a team conflict. Similarly, my love of learning inspires me to encourage a culture of curiosity and development within my organization. It's why I champion professional growth opportunities for my team and constantly seek ways to challenge myself and others to think differently.

Character strengths are more than tools; they're the foundation for building inclusive, resilient, and high-performing teams. When we understand our own strengths, we become more self-aware and intentional in how we show up. When we understand the strengths of our team members, we can harness their unique talents to drive collective success. It's about seeing people for their roles and their full potential—empowering them to bring their whole selves to work.

Let's start by unpacking the transformative power of character strengths and how, when harnessed effectively, they can create a workplace where everyone feels valued, empowered, and inspired to excel.

Harnessing Character Strengths for Dynamic Team Performance

Building on the understanding of character strengths and their potential to transform individuals and teams, the remainder of this chapter delves into actionable ways leaders can use strengths to address the *Billion Dollar Blind Spot* and foster diversity, inclusion, and belonging.

The Power of Strengths-Based Leadership

Imagine walking into a room where everyone feels seen, valued, and empowered to bring their best. Strengths-based leadership creates this kind of environment. It begins with a simple but profound belief: every person has unique strengths, and when leveraged effectively, these strengths can unlock extraordinary potential.

Leaders are supposed to be strength detectives—uncovering and celebrating the unique contributions of every team member. This means shifting the focus from fixing weaknesses to amplifying strengths. Research from

Gallup shows that people who use their strengths daily are six times more likely to be engaged at work. This translates into higher productivity, increased retention, and a healthier workplace culture for organizations.

In the context of addressing the *Billion Dollar Blind Spot*, strengths-based leadership is transformative. When people feel their strengths are recognized and celebrated, they're more likely to invest their energy and creativity into solving complex problems, driving innovation, and contributing to organizational success.

Building Inclusive Cultures Through Strengths

Strengths are inherently diverse. By recognizing this diversity, leaders can build teams that thrive on inclusion and belonging. Here's how:

1. **Valuing Diverse Strengths** In a male-dominated industry, it's easy for unconscious biases to shape the perception of what "strength" looks like. Strengths-based leadership challenges this notion by valuing contributions that may not traditionally be celebrated. For instance, a strength like humility might not immediately stand out in a high-pressure corporate environment, but it fosters collaboration and trust— qualities that drive long-term success.

Example: In a recent project, I worked with a team that initially overlooked the quieter members during brainstorming sessions. By identifying and naming their strengths—such as perspective and fairness—we created structured opportunities for their insights to shine. The result? A richer, more balanced approach to decision-making.

2. **Creating Psychological Safety** Belonging starts with psychological safety. When people feel safe to express their ideas, take risks, and show vulnerability, they're more likely to bring their authentic selves to work. Strengths-based leadership fosters this safety by framing feedback and challenges around what people are naturally good at, building confidence and resilience.

   Practical Tip: During one-on-one meetings, ask team members, "Which of your strengths do you feel is underutilized in your current role?" This simple question validates their talents and opens the door for meaningful conversations about alignment and growth.

3. **Strengths and Intersectionality** Strengths-based leadership also helps address the nuances of intersectionality—where race, gender, and other identities intersect to shape experiences. By focusing on individual strengths, leaders can create equitable opportunities

that honor the unique contributions of every person, regardless of their background.

Using Strengths to Foster Collaboration

Collaboration is about standing out in ways that complement the team's goals. When leaders align team members' strengths with their roles and responsibilities, they create a synergy that drives performance.

1. **Mapping Strengths to Roles** Start by conducting a team strengths assessment. Tools like the VIA Survey or Clifton Strengths can help identify individual and collective strengths. Once you have this data, align team members' strengths with tasks that energize and engage them.

   Example: On a recent project, a team member with a top strength in creativity was struggling with routine administrative tasks. Their engagement soared by reallocating those duties and giving them ownership of brainstorming and problem-solving initiatives, and the team benefited from their innovative ideas.

2. **Balancing Strengths** While playing to individual strengths is essential, it's equally important to balance them across the team. If everyone excels in ideation

but lacks execution, the team may generate endless ideas without tangible outcomes. As a leader, identify gaps and pair complementary strengths to build a well-rounded team.

3. **Encouraging Peer-to-Peer Recognition** Strengths-based collaboration thrives on mutual respect and appreciation. Create opportunities for team members to recognize and celebrate each other's strengths. This fosters belonging and reinforces a culture where everyone's contributions are valued.

    Practical Tip: Implement a "Strengths Spotlight" during team meetings where individuals share examples of how a colleague's strengths positively impacted a project.

Strengths and Leadership Development

Leaders who embrace their own strengths model authenticity and self-awareness, inspiring their teams to do the same. Here's how you can integrate strengths into your leadership journey:

1. **Self-Reflection** Regularly assess your own strengths and how they show up in your leadership style. Are you leveraging your strengths to inspire and guide your

team? Are there situations where your strengths might unintentionally become blind spots?

Example: My top strength, humor, helps me build rapport and diffuse tension. However, I've learned to balance this by ensuring it doesn't overshadow moments that require gravity and focus.

2. **Strengths-Based Feedback** Use strengths as a foundation for feedback. Instead of focusing on what's "wrong," highlight how a team member's strengths can be used to overcome challenges or seize opportunities.

3. **Encouraging Growth** Strengths evolve, and so should we. Encourage team members to explore and develop strengths they may not yet fully own. This boosts their confidence and creates a ripple effect of growth and adaptability.

Character strengths are more than individual traits; they're the building blocks of dynamic, inclusive, and high-performing teams. As leaders, it's our responsibility to uncover, celebrate, and cultivate these strengths—not just in ourselves, but in those we lead.

By embracing strengths-based leadership, you're not just addressing the *Billion Dollar Blind Spot* but redefining what success looks like. You're creating a culture where everyone has the opportunity to shine, contribute, and belong. And in doing so, you're unlocking a future of limitless potential—for your people, purpose, and profits.

So, here's my challenge to you: Start today. Take the VIA Survey or Clifton Strengths assessment and encourage your team to do the same. Use the results as a springboard for conversations, strategies, and initiatives that bring strengths to the forefront of your organization. Because when we lead with strengths, we lead with purpose—and that's where true transformation begins.

Strengths-Based Approach as a Catalyst for Transformation

The *Billion Dollar Blind Spot*—marked by disengagement, turnover, and missed opportunities—often stems from environments that fail to recognize and harness the full potential of their people. Strengths-based leadership changes this narrative. When leaders focus on amplifying individual and collective strengths, they create spaces where everyone feels valued, empowered, and motivated to contribute their best.

This approach is particularly powerful in fostering diversity and inclusion. Strengths are inherently unique, transcending traditional stereotypes and breaking down barriers of bias. By recognizing and celebrating the diverse strengths within our teams, we build cultures where all voices are heard, respected, and included. This is transformative for women and underrepresented groups—it shifts the focus from meeting outdated norms to thriving as their authentic selves, leveraging their strengths to drive meaningful impact.

Turning Strengths into Action for Inclusion and Growth

Strengths-based leadership provides a practical roadmap for transforming workplace culture into one of inclusion and growth. It's about taking the concept of individual strengths and putting it into action—empowering unique contributions, fostering belonging, and tackling disengagement at its root. By leveraging strengths strategically, leaders can drive innovation, build resilience, and create environments where everyone thrives. The following principles highlight how strengths-based leadership can become a catalyst for meaningful change.

1. **Empowering Unique Contributions**
A strengths-based lens helps leaders see individuals for their potential, not just their job titles. It's about recognizing that humility, empathy, or creativity are as valuable to team success as analytical or technical

skills. This shift in perspective unlocks talent that might otherwise go unnoticed, allowing diverse strengths to shine and contribute to collective goals.

2. **Building Inclusive Cultures**
   Strengths-based leadership inherently fosters belonging. When individuals see their unique qualities acknowledged and utilized, they feel an authentic connection to their work and their colleagues. This is the foundation of psychological safety, where diverse teams can collaborate, innovate, and grow without fear of judgment or exclusion.

3. **Addressing the Root Causes of Disengagement**
   Much of the disengagement in workplaces arises from employees feeling unseen or undervalued. By integrating strengths into leadership and team dynamics, we create environments where people see their contributions making a tangible difference. This sense of purpose and alignment is a powerful antidote to disengagement.

The journey to solving the *Billion Dollar Blind Spot* starts with a single step: recognizing that every team member holds untapped potential. As leaders, it's our responsibility to uncover and amplify that potential. Take action today—conduct a strengths assessment, open conversations about character strengths within your team, and commit to creating a culture where strengths drive success.

Imagine the impact of a workplace where everyone is empowered to bring their best selves to the table. Picture a team that thrives on diverse perspectives, fuels innovation through collaboration, and uplifts one another in pursuit of shared goals. This is the power of strengths-based leadership—a leadership that addresses the challenges we face and turns them into opportunities for growth, inclusion, and lasting success.

The future of work demands leaders who see beyond what is and envision what could be. By embracing character strengths, you're not just leading your team—you're transforming your organization and shaping a world where diversity and inclusion are not just ideals but realities. Lead with strengths, lead with purpose, and lead the way to a thriving future.

Coaching for Cultural Transformation

The greatest danger in times of turbulence is not the turbulence; it is to act with yesterday's logic.
—Peter Drucker

Let's explore the transformative power of intertwining personal resilience with the impact of coaching in organizational settings. My own journey serves as a testament to the profound influence coaching can have—not only in overcoming personal challenges but also in shaping the culture of entire organizations.

I recognize the pivotal role coaching has played throughout my life. I've had extensive experience coaching in sport, where guiding teams to work cohesively and push past limitations felt natural. Yet, for a long time, I lacked mentors and coaching in the realm of business and leadership. It wasn't until I sought out leadership and business coaches that I realized how transformative the process could be. This shift fundamentally changed the game for me, equipping me with tools, insights, and strategies to navigate the complexities of organizational leadership with confidence and clarity.

This lesson became even more profound as I embarked on my personal journey through resilience and determination. After a life-altering horse-riding accident that tested every facet of my endurance—physical, mental, and emotional—I discovered the invaluable role coaching plays in navigating self-doubt and fear. Through this crucible of adversity, I gained a deep understanding of the human spirit's capacity to overcome, adapt, and thrive.

Founding Empowered Women in Trades brought this appreciation to the forefront, highlighting coaching's role as a catalyst for both personal growth and cultural change. Through a blend of self-coaching practices and external mentorship, I honed my leadership, resilience, and empathy skills—qualities that have proven essential in driving meaningful and sustainable transformation in workplaces.

At its core, coaching for cultural transformation transcends individual development; it's about shaping a collective mindset rooted in inclusivity, collaboration, and authenticity. As a founder, I've learned firsthand how soul-testing the journey can be. Building something from the ground up is both exhilarating and exhausting, demanding a level of perseverance and self-leadership that often feels like a trial by fire. In these moments of profound challenge, I've come to understand the importance of self-leadership—the ability to guide yourself with clarity, resilience, and a steadfast belief in your vision, even when external validation feels scarce.

This journey has taught me that self-leadership is not about having all the answers but about cultivating the courage to ask the right questions, recalibrate when needed, and remain grounded in your values. This principle becomes the cornerstone for creating thriving workplaces when applied to cultural transformation. Organizations can unlock an unparalleled wave of creativity, innovation, and resilience by fostering a culture where every voice is heard, every perspective is valued, and every individual feels empowered to reach their full potential.

This isn't just about creating a "nice" workplace—it's a strategy for sustainable success and embracing the Respect Equality approach. When individuals feel seen, heard, and appreciated, they bring their full selves to work. They take ownership, embrace challenges, and collaborate in ways that drive organizations toward extraordinary outcomes. Coaching, both as a practice and a mindset, plays a pivotal role in unleashing this potential, turning adversity into opportunity and individuality into collective strength. To drive meaningful organizational change, leaders must transition from traditional managerial roles to becoming coaches—guides who inspire, empower, and nurture their teams' potential.

Coaching for cultural transformation is more than a developmental tool; it is a strategic approach to shifting mindsets, breaking down barriers, and building inclusive environments. Through personalized support and guidance, coaching encourages self-awareness and fosters openness to diversity, enabling individuals to confidently challenge entrenched norms and adapt to change. By cultivating empathy and resilience, coaching creates a foundation for leaders to champion diversity and inclusion initiatives authentically and effectively.

When leaders embrace their role as coaches, they guide individuals and shape the collective culture. Coaching empowers teams to navigate adversity, collaborate with intention, and contribute their unique perspectives and talents to the organization's success. This cultural shift ensures every member feels valued and understood, unleashing creativity, innovation, and resilience that drive sustainable growth and transformation.

Transforming workplace culture requires more than policies; it demands a holistic approach that integrates leadership, coaching, and intentional action. Adopting a coaching mindset is one of the most powerful ways for leaders to drive this transformation.

When leaders step into the role of coaches, they do more than manage tasks or oversee performance. They actively shape their teams' mindsets, behaviors, and attitudes, aligning them with cultural values that prioritize well-being, diversity, and collaboration. Coaching empowers leaders to guide their teams through change, address resistance with empathy, and foster an environment where everyone feels valued and heard.

Everything we have discussed—addressing biases, building psychological safety, fostering inclusivity, and embracing diversity of thought—is interconnected. Coaching serves as the glue that binds these elements together, offering leaders the tools to embed these principles into the fabric of their organizations. Through coaching, leaders can unlock the potential of their teams, creating cultures where innovation thrives and employees feel empowered to contribute their best.

Coaching ensures that cultural transformation is sustainable, deeply rooted in the practices and behaviors of the organization and aligned with the evolving expectations of today's workforce. By embracing the dual roles of leader and coach, executives can pave the way for a future where workplace cultures are not only productive but also equitable, inclusive, and resilient.

By tailoring guidance to the unique needs of each individual, coaching enables leaders to nurture both strengths and areas for growth. This personalized support fosters skill development, adaptability, and the mindset required to thrive in an inclusive and resilient culture. Leaders who adopt a coaching mindset do more than guide—they empower their teams, building collaboration, trust, and a shared purpose.

Ultimately, coaching transforms leaders into champions of cultural change. It bridges the gap between aspiration and action, fostering a workplace where inclusivity and innovation thrive. But to truly succeed in this role, leaders must master a multifaceted approach—one that integrates **intellectual intelligence (IQ)**, **emotional intelligence (EQ)**, **artificial intelligence quotient (AIQ)**, and **spiritual intelligence (SQ)**. Together, these dimensions form the foundation for transformative leadership that drives both individual and organizational growth.

Introducing the Framework of IQ, EQ, AIQ, and SQ in Coaching for Cultural Transformation

In coaching for cultural transformation, a comprehensive framework that integrates Intellectual Quotient (IQ), Emotional Quotient (EQ), Artificial Intelligence Quotient (AIQ), and Spiritual Quotient (SQ) provides the foundation for transformative leadership and sustainable organizational change. Each component contributes distinct strengths, enabling leaders to foster a culture of inclusivity, empathy, and resilience.

1. **Intellectual Quotient (IQ):**

   IQ represents critical cognitive abilities for strategic thinking, problem-solving, and navigating complexity. Leadership today is not about seeing challenges as complications to be avoided but as complexities to be embraced. Effective leaders use their intellectual capabilities to guide their teams through ambiguity, fostering clarity and direction. By embracing complexity, leaders can identify growth opportunities, design innovative strategies, and support their teams in adapting to change confidently and purposefully.

2. **Emotional Quotient (EQ):**

   EQ encompasses the self-awareness, self-regulation, empathy, motivation, and interpersonal skills essential for effective leadership. One of the most transformative lessons I've learned is the ability to empathize deeply with others without absorbing their struggles as my own. This balance allows leaders to provide meaningful support without compromising their own emotional well-being. By cultivating EQ, leaders create environments where individuals feel valued, understood, and empowered to contribute authentically. This emotional grounding strengthens trust and collaboration, driving cultural transformation.

3. **Artificial Intelligence Quotient (AIQ):**

   AIQ represents a leader's ability to understand, engage with, and leverage artificial intelligence in decision-making and organizational processes. In today's rapidly evolving landscape, leaders must embrace AI and use it to enhance human potential rather than replace it. AIQ involves knowing how to integrate AI tools ethically and effectively, ensuring they augment creativity, innovation, and productivity within teams. By balancing AI's capabilities with human values and judgment, leaders foster a future-ready culture that aligns with the broader goals of inclusivity and growth.

4. **Spiritual Quotient (SQ):**

   SQ refers to the ability to align actions and decisions with one's values, beliefs, and moral principles. This quotient drives purpose, authenticity, and ethical leadership. Leaders with a high SQ inspire trust and meaning, fostering a sense of shared purpose across the organization. Connecting day-to-day actions to a larger vision and values creates a culture of integrity and social responsibility that supports long-term success.

The Synergy of the Four Components

When leaders integrate IQ, EQ, AIQ, and SQ into their approach, they create a powerful synergy that drives individual growth and collective transformation. This framework equips leaders to navigate the complexities of modern workplaces, foster emotional resilience, harness technological advancements, and lead with integrity and purpose. Together, these dimensions form the cornerstone of coaching for cultural transformation, addressing the *Billion Dollar Blind Spot* through inclusive, innovative, and ethically aligned leadership.

The Integration of IQ, EQ, AIQ, and SQ in Coaching for Cultural Transformation

Integrating IQ, EQ, AIQ, and SQ in coaching for cultural transformation provides leaders with a comprehensive framework to drive meaningful organizational change. Each dimension contributes unique strengths, creating a holistic approach to navigating the complexities of modern leadership and fostering an environment of inclusivity, empathy, and innovation.

1. **IQ (Intellectual Quotient):**
   IQ equips leaders with the cognitive abilities necessary

for strategic insight, analytical thinking, and innovative problem-solving. Effective leaders use IQ not to complicate issues but to navigate complexity, breaking down challenges into actionable steps. By leveraging their intellectual capabilities, leaders develop strategies that address cultural transformation with precision and foresight, fostering organizational resilience and adaptability.

2. **EQ (Emotional Quotient):**
   EQ encompasses self-awareness, emotional regulation, empathy, and social skills, enabling leaders to connect authentically with their teams. One transformative lesson I've learned is the importance of empathizing with others without absorbing their struggles as my own. This balance is critical for fostering trust and maintaining emotional boundaries, essential to leading with empathy and compassion. EQ empowers leaders to navigate interpersonal dynamics effectively, cultivating a workplace culture where collaboration and inclusivity thrive.

3. **AIQ (Artificial Intelligence Quotient):**
   AIQ represents the ability to understand, engage with, and leverage artificial intelligence to augment human potential. In today's fast-evolving workplaces,

leaders must integrate AI thoughtfully to enhance decision-making, streamline processes, and drive innovation. However, AIQ also involves ethical considerations—leaders must ensure that AI applications align with organizational values, uphold inclusivity, and promote equity. By balancing AI's capabilities with human judgment, leaders position their organizations to thrive in a future-ready and inclusive manner.

4. **SQ (Spiritual Quotient):**
SQ reflects a leader's ability to align their actions with values, purpose, and moral principles. It promotes authenticity, integrity, and a sense of shared vision, which are vital for leading with trust and inspiring others. Leaders with high SQ connect organizational objectives to a deeper purpose, fostering a sense of meaning and belonging within their teams. This alignment ensures that cultural transformation efforts are grounded in ethics and social responsibility, amplifying their impact on the organization and beyond.

Harnessing the Collective Power of IQ, EQ, AIQ, and SQ

By integrating IQ, EQ, AIQ, and SQ, leaders are equipped to navigate the multifaceted challenges of cultural transformation. This comprehensive approach fosters clarity, emotional intelligence, technological aptitude, and moral grounding, empowering leaders to create environments where individuals and teams thrive.

A defining moment for me personally came when I transitioned from accounting to organizational psychology—a path that required me to apply IQ for problem-solving, EQ for understanding interpersonal dynamics, and SQ to align my career with my values and passions. More recently, incorporating AIQ into my leadership approach has allowed me to embrace technological advancements while remaining committed to inclusivity and empathy.

Through implementing coaching programs, I've witnessed firsthand how these dimensions profoundly impact team dynamics and individual well-being. Coaching, rooted in IQ, EQ, AIQ, and SQ, enables leaders to foster authenticity, resilience, and a growth mindset within their organizations.

Daniel Goleman, a pioneer of Emotional Intelligence, emphasizes that EQ—comprising self-awareness, empathy, and social skills—is critical for effective leadership and interpersonal relationships. Meanwhile, Stephen Covey's work on Spiritual Intelligence highlights the importance of values-based leadership in enhancing integrity and vision. By complementing these with IQ's cognitive rigor and AIQ's technological acumen, leaders can address the *Billion Dollar Blind Spot* through a multifaceted lens, balancing innovation with inclusivity and empathy.

This integrated framework underscores the transformative power of coaching to create workplaces where diverse talents are valued, cultures are inclusive, and organizations achieve sustainable success.

Integrating IQ, EQ, AIQ, and SQ into Coaching for Cultural Transformation

Integrating **IQ (Intellectual Quotient)**, **EQ (Emotional Quotient)**, **AIQ (Artificial Intelligence Quotient)**, and **SQ (Spiritual Quotient)** into coaching for cultural transformation provides a holistic framework for leaders to drive meaningful and sustainable change. Each dimension complements the others, addressing the intellectual, emotional, technological, and ethical aspects of leadership required to build resilient, inclusive, and innovative organizational cultures.

- **IQ (Intellectual Quotient):**
  High IQ equips leaders with the cognitive tools to navigate complex strategic challenges and innovate effectively. IQ isn't about overcomplicating problems but embracing complexity to create clear, actionable

solutions. For example, **Jeff Bezos**, renowned for his analytical and strategic thinking, leveraged his high IQ to revolutionize e-commerce and logistics, driving Amazon's global success while managing complex operations.

- **EQ (Emotional Quotient):**
EQ enables leaders to foster empathy, understanding, and effective communication, creating an emotionally intelligent environment that supports psychological well-being. I've learned the importance of empathizing with others without taking on their struggles personally—an essential skill for maintaining clarity and emotional balance. **Oprah Winfrey** exemplifies EQ, connecting deeply with her audience and team, creating trust and understanding while driving transformative conversations in media and philanthropy.

- **AIQ (Artificial Intelligence Quotient):**
AIQ reflects a leader's ability to understand and integrate AI technologies into their decision-making and operations. Leaders with high AIQ use technology to enhance innovation, improve workflows, and make data-informed decisions. However, AIQ also involves ethical considerations, such as addressing biases in AI systems and ensuring technological solutions align with

organizational values. For example, AIQ is critical in industries adopting AI for predictive analytics or process automation, where leaders must balance technological efficiency with ethical responsibility and inclusivity.

- **SQ (Spiritual Quotient):**
  SQ focuses on values-driven leadership, aligning actions with purpose, integrity, and vision. It enables leaders to foster a sense of shared meaning within their organizations, inspiring teams to connect their work with a larger mission. **The Dalai Lama** exemplifies SQ by embodying compassion and ethical leadership, guiding actions with moral clarity to promote peace and understanding globally.

A Holistic Approach for Cultural Transformation

By integrating IQ, EQ, AIQ, and SQ into their leadership approach, leaders can address the multidimensional challenges of cultural transformation:

1. **IQ** provides the cognitive capacity to design innovative solutions and strategic roadmaps.
2. **EQ** nurtures the interpersonal and emotional connections necessary for collaborative success.

3. **AIQ** equips leaders to harness technology respon-
   sibly and effectively, ensuring organizations remain
   future-ready.
4. **SQ** anchors leadership in values and purpose, fostering
   trust and ethical decision-making.

This framework fosters a workplace culture where
inclusivity, creativity, and resilience thrive. For instance,
a leader navigating gender respect initiatives can use IQ
to analyze systemic barriers, EQ to engage with diverse
perspectives, AIQ to deploy equitable technological
solutions, and SQ to align actions with organizational
values. Together, these elements create a foundation for
lasting cultural transformation that addresses the *Billion
Dollar Blind Spot* through a focus on a Respect Equality
approach and positions organizations as leaders in innovation and inclusivity.

Breaking the Double Bind: Creating Equitable Workplaces

We cannot solve our problems with the same thinking we used when we created them.
—Albert Einstein

In male-dominated industries, women often find themselves entangled in a pernicious phenomenon known as the double bind. This occurs when they receive conflicting feedback—told to be more confident, yet criticized for being too assertive or aggressive when they are. This contradictory feedback creates a paralyzing bind, leaving women feeling stuck and unsure how to navigate workplace dynamics effectively. Acknowledging the existence of the double bind is not about placing blame on any individual but recognizing the systemic challenges that perpetuate this phenomenon.

I've experienced this firsthand. With a naturally strong and powerful voice, I'm often accused of "yelling," even when speaking firmly or passionately. The irony isn't lost on me—it's commonplace for men to yell across the site without a second thought on construction sites. Yet, when a woman like me speaks with strength and conviction, it's perceived differently. I've also been in situations where the feedback has been the opposite: when I've softened my voice or tone, I've been told I'm not standing my ground or asserting my leadership effectively. This paradox illustrates the double bind perfectly—women are expected to strike an impossible balance, where being too strong is seen as a flaw, yet not strong enough is equally criticized.

These experiences underscore the importance of addressing the double bind. It's not just about individual behaviors or feedback but dismantling the systemic norms that uphold these contradictory expectations. By recognizing and challenging these biases, we can create workplaces where women are valued for their voices—whether they speak softly, firmly, or passionately—without being boxed into impossible expectations.

By educating ourselves, our leadership teams, and managers about the double bind, we can start to dismantle its effects and create a more equitable workplace culture. One effective strategy is offering leadership training tailored to address the double bind. This training equips women with the tools and skills needed to recognize and navigate these challenges effectively. It empowers them to assert themselves confidently while also providing strategies to address feedback that may be rooted in gender biases.

Additionally, it's crucial to educate male leaders on the existence of the double bind and equip them with the tools to recognize and address it when it arises. Often, male leaders may unknowingly perpetuate the double bind, not out of malice but due to a lack of awareness about its existence and impact. By fostering awareness and understanding among all organization members, we can work together to challenge and dismantle the barriers that hold women back in the workplace.

For example, consider a scenario where a female team member is presenting a proposal during a leadership meeting. She confidently outlines her ideas, speaking with authority and conviction. After the meeting, a male leader comments that while her ideas were strong, she came across as "too aggressive" in her delivery. The same leader later praises a male colleague for presenting his ideas with "confidence and decisiveness," even though his delivery mirrored hers. This discrepancy highlights the double bind in action—where women are penalized for behaviors that are celebrated in men.

To address such situations, male leaders must first cultivate awareness of how unconscious biases may influence their perceptions and feedback. They can start by reflecting on whether similar behaviors are evaluated differently based on gender. In the example above, the male leader could ask himself: "Would I have given the same feedback to a male colleague who presented with the same tone and energy?" This self-reflection helps uncover biases that might otherwise go unnoticed.

Moreover, male leaders can actively challenge the double bind by acknowledging and celebrating diverse communication styles, ensuring feedback focuses on the substance of the message rather than subjective perceptions of delivery. For instance, instead of criticizing the female team member's "aggressiveness," the leader could offer constructive feedback by saying: "Your points were well-articulated and compelling. Let's discuss further refining the delivery to maximize impact." This approach validates her contribution without reinforcing gendered stereotypes.

Organizationally, implementing training programs that include role-playing exercises and real-world scenarios can help male leaders better understand how the double bind manifests and learn strategies to address it effectively. By creating safe spaces for dialogue and education, organizations can empower male leaders to become allies, actively working to dismantle the systemic barriers contributing to gender inequality. When male leaders understand and address the double bind, it sets the tone for an equitable workplace where women can confidently thrive without fear of being unfairly judged for how they express themselves.

Ultimately, by proactively addressing the double bind and creating a culture that values and supports gender equality, we can foster an environment where leaders—regardless of gender—can lead authentically. The goal is to cultivate a workplace where individuals feel empowered to bring their full selves to their roles, free from the constraints of outdated stereotypes or contradictory expectations. This means celebrating diverse leadership styles, encouraging open dialogue, and ensuring constructive and equitable feedback. Organizations benefit from greater creativity, collaboration, and a deeper sense of trust and respect across teams when leaders can lean into their authentic strengths without fear of being unfairly judged. This cultural shift is not just about equity; it's a strategic imperative for fostering innovation and driving sustainable success.

Next, as leaders we can use the ladder of inference to challenge our assumptions and test the validity of our beliefs. This involves consciously climbing down the ladder to the bottom rung, where observable data and facts reside. By examining the evidence in front of us and going wide on collecting evidence without filtering it through preconceived notions or biases, we can gain a clearer understanding of the situation and make more informed decisions. This involves ensuring we are challenging ourselves to source evidence outside of our normal scope.

To give you an example, let's consider a scenario

where a team leader is evaluating a team member's performance, Sarah. The leader notices that Sarah has missed several project deadlines and jumps to the assumption that she is lazy or uncommitted to her work. This initial interpretation represents the top rung of the ladder of inference, where the leader's beliefs and biases influence their perception of the situation.

To challenge this assumption and test its validity, the leader decides to climb down the ladder to the bottom rung, where observable data and facts reside. Instead of relying solely on their initial impression, the leader takes a step back and collects evidence from various sources. They review Sarah's project reports, examine communication records, and gather feedback from other team members and stakeholders.

During this process, the leader uncovers that Sarah has been navigating significant personal challenges outside of work, including health issues and family responsibilities, which have affected her ability to meet deadlines. Beyond these personal difficulties, the leader also identifies systemic issues within the team, such as delays in colleagues providing Sarah with necessary information and resources, further compounding her struggles to stay on schedule.

Despite these obstacles, the leader recognizes that Sarah has consistently demonstrated unwavering dedication and initiative, often contributing innovative ideas and effective solutions to team projects. By piecing together a more comprehensive view of the situation, the leader acknowledges that Sarah's performance issues are not solely a reflection of her individual circumstances but are also influenced by broader team dynamics that need to be addressed.

By seeking additional evidence and broadening their perspective beyond initial assumptions, the leader uncovers a clearer understanding of Sarah's situation. Rather than attributing her performance issues solely to individual challenges, the leader identifies deeper workflow inefficiencies affecting the entire team.

Delays in colleagues providing essential information, unclear communication channels, and a lack of structured support systems emerge as systemic problems within the organization. Sarah's challenges were merely where these issues became most visible. The leader realizes that her performance is not a standalone issue but a symptom of larger workflow inefficiencies that hinder the team's overall effectiveness.

This broader understanding shifts the focus from Sarah as the problem to addressing systemic inefficiencies, paving the way for a more collaborative and sustainable solution that benefits the entire team.

Armed with this newfound insight, the leader is better equipped to address the issue constructively, delving deeper into the root causes rather than treating the symptoms. Through further investigation, they identify underlying issues such as unclear role expectations, inefficiencies in communication, and a lack of cross-functional accountability that have exacerbated Sarah's challenges.

Rather than reprimand Sarah for perceived shortcomings, the leader approaches her empathetically, recognizing that her struggles reflect broader systemic problems. They work collaboratively to offer tailored support, such as redistributing responsibilities, clarifying deliverables, and ensuring that necessary resources are accessible. Flexibility in her workload is not merely a short-term solution; it becomes part of a larger effort to improve team workflows and create more equitable distribution of tasks.

This shift in perspective strengthens the leader's relationship with Sarah by demonstrating genuine understanding and commitment to her success. Beyond that, it fosters a culture of collaboration, where team members feel safe to share challenges and collectively address inefficiencies. By tackling the root causes of the issues, the leader empowers Sarah and drives long-term improvements in team cohesion and organizational effectiveness.

Moreover, active listening plays a crucial role in fostering empathy and understanding within teams. Leaders who practice attentive listening focus not only on the words being spoken but also on their colleagues' emotions, tone, and underlying messages. This level of engagement allows leaders to move beyond surface-level interactions and truly understand the perspectives and needs of their team members.

Unchecked biases, such as affinity bias (the tendency to favor those who are similar to us), can have significant costs in the workplace. When leaders fail to listen and challenge their biases actively, it can result in missed opportunities, reduced team morale, and a stifled exchange of ideas. These biases often perpetuate workplace inequities and contribute to the *Billion Dollar Blind Spot* by driving disengagement, lowering productivity, and fostering cultures where only certain voices are heard.

Active listening and perspective-taking align with Barbara Fredrickson's *Broaden and Build Theory*, which highlights how positive emotions, such as those generated through genuine empathy and inclusivity, expand our cognitive resources and foster resilience. Leaders unlock the potential for innovation and creative problem-solving by creating environments where diverse perspectives are valued. These actions don't just address immediate challenges—they cultivate long-term organizational health and adaptability.

Incorporating this approach can dismantle barriers created by bias and transform organizational culture. Embracing diversity of thought, actively engaging with different viewpoints, and prioritizing active listening fosters innovation, creativity, and collaboration. When leaders commit to these practices, they not only strengthen their teams but also contribute to a more equitable and effective workplace, directly tackling the *Billion Dollar Blind Spot* by unlocking the full potential of their workforce.

Conclusion
Embracing the Journey

The journey to transform our organizations and ourselves is not easy, but it is essential. We create workplaces where everyone can thrive by embracing vulnerability, fostering trust, and committing to inclusivity. Together, we can transform the *Billion Dollar Blind Spot* into an opportunity for innovation, engagement, and sustainable success.

As we honor the legacy of those who came before us, it's vital to recognize that the fight for progress has entered a new chapter. The battles of the past fought with courage and resilience have paved the way for today's opportunity to create lasting change. Now, it is time to set aside the weapons of division and discord and embrace a new paradigm one rooted in respect, understanding, and unity. This shift is not just a moral imperative but a strategic necessity to address the *Billion Dollar Blind Spot* that no one is talking about: the cost of disengagement, inequality, and untapped potential within our organizations.

By connecting on the fundamental level of our shared humanity, we transcend the barriers that divide us. We move beyond surface-level diversity metrics to foster environments where inclusivity is not a checkbox but a deeply embedded value. That's what the Respect Equality approach is all about. When we recognize and celebrate each person's unique identities and perspectives, we unlock our teams' collective power. Within these spaces of respect and equality, innovation thrives, resilience strengthens, and collaboration becomes transformative.

The path is not easy. My own journey of learning to walk again after my life-altering horse-riding accident exemplifies this truth. Each step I took, quite literally, was fraught with challenges and setbacks. There were moments when I stumbled, fell, and felt the weight of frustration and despair. Yet, through those failures, I gained the insights and strength necessary to take the next step forward.

In those moments of struggle, I learned to refine my approach, listen to my body, and trust the process. Similarly, as leaders, failure offers us the opportunity to reflect, adjust our strategies, and build resilience. Just as I had to confront the vulnerability of starting over, leaders must confront the vulnerabilities inherent in embracing failure and uncertainty.

Through this lens, failure becomes a powerful teacher that equips us with the tools to lead with greater empathy, courage, and authenticity. By embracing failure as part of the journey, we grow as individuals and create environments where our teams feel safe to take risks, innovate, and learn, ultimately driving collective progress and success.

The *Billion Dollar Blind Spot* is the neglect of inclusive leadership and the untapped potential within us all. This issue more than just about inequality; it's about the cost of failing to honor our shared humanity. That's why I named my approach the Respect Equality approach—because it's not just about enforced equality by artificial metrics, but genuine respect.

We stand at a crossroads, where the call for respect and equality is louder than ever. This is not more than a moral imperative; it's a strategic necessity for building thriving, innovative organizations. Inclusive leadership must become the cornerstone of our corporate evolution, ensuring that every individual has equal access to opportunities, resources, and rights irrespective of gender identity.

To the men, I urge you to reclaim the full spectrum of your humanity. Strength does not come from suppressing vulnerability but from embracing it. Lead with empathy, authenticity, and the courage to challenge outdated norms of masculinity. Be the champions of a new paradigm, where respect and equality are the measure of true leadership.

To the women, your voice, resilience, and unwavering pursuit of progress are the guiding light for this transformation. Stand tall and claim your space unapologetically. Continue to challenge the barriers, support one another, and lead with both strength and grace. Together, we can redefine what leadership looks like and ensure that no voice is left unheard.

Men and women, yin and yang, together we hold the power to bring balance to the corporate world. Only through unity, acknowledging our differences, celebrating our unique strengths, and working as equals can we usher in a new era of workplace culture. This is the foundation of deep respect and equality, where psychological well-being thrives, and every individual can bring their whole self to work.

The time to act is now. The silent *Billion Dollar Blind Spot* can no longer be ignored. It is within our grasp to create a future where workplaces become places of empowerment, belonging, and innovation a future where humanity and success are not at odds but intertwined.

The future is ours to create.

Will you answer the call?

SILVERSMITH
PRESS

Serves new and emerging authors
to help them write, publish, and promote their books.
Are you ready to share your story?

Visit us!
www.silversmithpress.com

www.ingramcontent.com/pod-product-compliance
Lightning Source LLC
Chambersburg PA
CBHW041732200326
41518CB00019B/2572